Beneath the
Tip of the Iceberg

Improving English and
Understanding U.S. Cultural Patterns

DARLA K. DEARDORFF
KAY M. BOWMAN

Ann Arbor
The University of Michigan Press

Copyright © by the University of Michigan 2011
All rights reserved
Published in the United States of America
The University of Michigan Press
Manufactured in the United States of America

∞ Printed on acid-free paper

ISBN-13: 978-0-472-03333-1

2014   2013   2012   2011   4   3   2   1

Acknowledgments

There are many people who are involved in the publication of a book. We wish to thank the persons who contributed stories to this book—especially Charlotte, Wayne, Shirley, Arlene, Edith, Marlene, Kate, Kimberly, Reginald, Julu, Becky, Helen, and Tonu. Deep appreciation also goes to Devin Bowman, Duane Deardorff, Kaylee Deardorff, and Shaun Deardorff. Appreciation also goes to those who reviewed this text including Ina Baumann, Edith Cowper, Suzanne Panferov, Adriana Arijuo, Ana Guerrero, and Karin Abell. We also want to express gratitude to the University of Michigan Press for working with us on the publication of this text.

We also want to acknowledge the generosity of "This I Believe" for allowing use of the stories that appear on these pages: 14, 27, 42, 49, 68, 93, 101, 114, 119, 132, 152, 158, 171, 183. The unedited essays appear with permission from "This I Believe." Essays are held in the copyright of the original author, part of the This I Believe Essay Collection found at www.thisibelieve.org. Copyright © 2005–2011 by This I Believe, Inc. Reprinted with permission.

Contents

To the Student

Have you ever wondered why people behave the way they do? Have you found that you can speak another language but still don't always understand the cultural behavior of the people who speak that language? Do you ever wish you could more fully explore another culture with someone from that culture who could be your cultural guide?

Understanding another culture can be quite difficult. What you see on TV or in movies often does not give a true idea about the culture. Books about another culture often describe different aspects of culture such as pop culture or history or geography. But to learn more about another culture, it is important to meet people from that culture. In this book, you will meet 28 real Americans from many different backgrounds and from all over the United States—20 different states plus Washington, DC, and Puerto Rico. These Americans will share with you what is important to them, and as you read their stories, you will come to see some of the values and beliefs that are important to many U.S. Americans. These stories are written in the individuals' own words, using their English.

The main purpose of this book is to help you better understand one part of U.S. American culture—beyond what is seen on TV and beyond holidays, food, music, history, and pop culture. By understanding more deeply about another culture, you can begin to understand better how culture influences behavior that you encounter. Learning another language is also about learning the culture—and to truly understand another culture, it is important to see it from the others' perspectives, not just through our own eyes. In better understanding American culture, it is important to gain a deeper understanding of your own culture too. You will find that many of the activities will ask you to think about both your own culture and U.S. American culture. So, why is it important to gain this understanding of American culture? Through a deeper cultural understanding, you will hopefully be able to get along even better with Americans and be more successful in your interactions. Getting along together means that we begin to break down walls that keep us apart and helps bring peace to our world.

The other purpose of this book is to help you practice and improve your English. Remember that the stories are written by real Americans in their own words—so you will be reading English as a native speaker writes it. In addition to the stories, which provide you with reading practice, you will also find exercises that will help you learn new vocabulary. Writing and speaking activities help you think more not only about the story you read but also about important beliefs and values in U.S. American culture. During these activities, you will be asked to work in a pair with another student or in small groups. Speaking with others will not only help you practice your own English but it will help other students learn more about your culture too. An important activity following each story asks you to apply and practice what you have learned by actually interacting with U.S. Americans in your community. (If you don't know too many Americans yet, your teacher can help you know how to meet them.)

As you go through this book, you are encouraged to keep a vocabulary notebook to keep track of new words you learn. You are also encouraged to write journal entries about your interactions with U.S. Americans—what you learn from them about the culture of the U.S. and what you learn about your own culture. This is a very important part of the cultural learning process. The Notes Section (pages 202–10) provides a place for your reflections after you finish each unit. Unit 15 also offers an opportunity to develop an action plan that will help you be more successful in your interactions with U.S. Americans.

A word about the Americans whose stories are featured in this book. You will be reading stories by black and white Americans, by Asian Americans, by Native Americans, by Hispanic Americans, by an Arab American, and by Americans of mixed races and ethnicities. Some are younger and some are older. About half of them live in cities and urban areas, and the other half live in small towns and rural areas. The stories are not unique to the geographic area highlighted in each story, but, rather, the geographic area *is simply a means for organizing this book*. It is important to remember that these Americans are from all over the United States—not just from a few places—so you'll have the chance to meet quite a few Americans from around the country. Their stories represent cultural *patterns* found in U.S. American culture. Through their stories, you will learn about what is important to many U.S. Americans and the underlying values that may impact Americans' behavior. Please remember that these stories represent cultural patterns and that not all Americans will believe or feel the same way. That's why it's so important that you get to know individual Americans and that you build relationships with them. Each unit contains questions that you can ask U.S. Americans as a way to get to know individual U.S. citizens.

Learning about other cultures is a lifelong journey. This book is one step in that journey—enjoy!

An Introduction for the Teacher

A story is told of six blind men and an elephant. The blind men asked, "What is the elephant like?" and they began to touch its body. One of them said, "It is like a pillar." This blind man had only touched its leg. Another man said, "The elephant is like a husking basket." This person had only touched its ears. Similarly, he who touched its trunk or its belly talked of it differently. In the same way, culture must be experienced from different perspectives to gain a richer, deeper understanding of that culture. This textbook provides a myriad of authentic perspectives from U.S. Americans on their own culture.

Overview

How do we as teachers teach U.S. American culture to our students? What specifically should we teach about culture? How can we go beyond teaching history, literature, and geography to helping our students truly begin to understand U.S. Americans as they interact with them on a daily basis? Specifically, how can we teach cultural values to our students? This book was written with these questions in mind.

Why are cultural values so important to teach? As teachers, we know that culture and language are intertwined. Too often, though, when we teach about U.S. American culture, we tend to teach the proverbial "tip of the cultural iceberg"—holidays, music, food, history, geography, pop culture, and so on. We also know that we need to teach what is beneath that proverbial tip—the part of U.S. American culture that is often difficult for our students to see and understand. This textbook addresses the parts of U.S. American culture that are hard to see and teach—the beliefs and values of the American people. Featured in this textbook are the stories of 28 Americans from all over the United States who represent a wide variety of cultures, races, ages, and backgrounds. The book includes stories from African Americans, Asian Americans, Caucasian Americans, Hispanic Americans, Native Americans, an Arab American, and Americans of mixed races and ethnicities. These Americans represent men and women, younger and older people, rural and urban lifestyles. Their personal stories have not been simplified in any way; each person's story is told in his or her own words. It's as if students will have visits from 28 different Americans, each sharing something that is important to them culturally and, in so doing, providing a more holistic view of U.S. American culture. This textbook is one of the first to offer this unique way in which to address these deeper culturally conditioned values—through authentic voices representing the rich diversity within the United States.

ESL students' in-depth questions about U.S. American culture, which no cultural textbook to date seemed to address, inspired this textbook. For example, my students would ask questions about what their cultural textbook really meant in terms of the daily lives of U.S. Americans, if it were possible to meet U.S. Americans who could actually talk about what was important to them, and what life was like for them growing up. My students really wanted to know more about U.S. Americans' perspectives on deeper issues such as diversity in the United States, relations among different races, how U.S. Americans felt about immigrants in their communities, how aspects of U.S. American culture had changed over time, and why U.S. Americans behaved in certain ways (for example, why do some U.S. Americans not take care of their older parents, why do many young U.S. Americans leave home at age 18, and so on). This textbook grew out of these conversations and is one response to students' desire to learn more about U.S. American culture.

Student feedback was invaluable in the development of this textbook. One of the authors met with students in several different focus groups during the development of this textbook, and possible ideas and formats were discussed. Through these discussions, as well as in one-on-one conversations with students, we found that students wanted to understand more about what U.S. Americans value so that they could better understand U.S. Americans' behaviors and, ultimately, be more successful in their interactions with U.S. Americans in their communities. They wanted to know and understand more about U.S. Americans' experiences, especially those from different parts of the United States. Since these students are based in North Carolina, they were quite curious about what Americans are like in different regions of the United States and not just those living in their community. The students wanted to go beyond what they learned at an abstract level in cultural textbooks and were interested in practical examples of how U.S. cultural values impact the daily lives of average U.S. Americans, not just those they read about in books, magazines, and newspapers.

It is important to point out that because U.S. Americans come from many different ethnic backgrounds and because the country is so big, it is not possible to define an "average American" or to assume that any particular cultural value is shared by all Americans. We do not want students to generalize or stereotype what an "average American" believes. Rather, by including stories from a diverse group of Americans representing a variety of ethnic groups, ages, and geographic regions of the country, we hope to broaden our students' perspectives. The 28 personal stories featured in this textbook have been selected to illustrate both the common cultural values and the individual diversity of U.S. Americans.

A note about terminology: Throughout this book, you will often see the term *U.S. American culture*. This is an intentional reference to strive to be more culturally sensitive since ESL students are often quick to point out that *American culture* can also include all cultures in South, Central, and North America. Nonetheless, in this book, *American* and *U.S. American* are used interchangeably, and any references to *American* culture refer to the culture of the United States. Realizing that there is much diversity within American culture as well, this textbook focuses on the major patterns found within U.S. American culture.

Purpose and Audience

This textbook serves to introduce students to the deeper levels of American culture and provides a stimulating springboard for further discussions among students regarding culture and understanding others, beyond history or holidays. The main purpose of this textbook is to help students gain a deeper understanding of U.S. Americans beyond what they may see portrayed on TV or in movies—in order to be more effective and appropriate in their interactions with Americans. This textbook will ultimately help students hone their intercultural competence (discussed in more detail on pages xxii–xxix).

At the core of the book are 28 authentic stories told by Americans from around the United States. Each story was selected in an attempt to illustrate *patterns* found in U.S. American culture. The stories provide examples of cultural values and personal beliefs that may be important not just to the author of the story but also to many U.S. Americans throughout the United States, although certainly not to all U.S. Americans, given the diversity found in this culture. In some cases, broad cultural patterns are repeated in different stories from Americans with different backgrounds who are living in different parts of the United States. Together, these stories create a more holistic and in-depth understanding of U.S. American culture and Americans.

Writing and speaking activities related to each story have been designed to help students explore these underlying values and beliefs, those in their own cultures and in U.S. American culture. Specifically, activities have been developed at the end of each story to encourage students to engage with U.S. Americans in their communities so that they can continue their cultural learning in the community in which they live, as well as to practice speaking English with fluent English speakers. Through these readings and activities, it is our hope that students will gain deeper insights into the underlying cultural values of U.S. Americans and, in so doing, will begin to better understand the contexts of Americans' behavior and actions. Ultimately, such understanding will hopefully ease students' transition of living in the United States.

This textbook is intended primarily for adult non-native speakers of English at the high-intermediate to advanced level who are living in the United States, although this could also be adapted to those students learning English in other countries. It could also be used by college students who desire to learn more about U.S. American culture. While this is primarily a textbook that teaches students about culture, it is also designed to help improve students' reading, writing, and speaking skills, and to expand their vocabularies.

Organization and Content

We have divided the material in this textbook into fifteen units. The first two units introduce students to the overall diversity (Unit 1) and underlying cultural values (Unit 2) of the United States. The remaining thirteen units in the textbook are then organized by geographic region, *solely to show that stories come from many parts of the United States, and not just one location within the country.* Most units contain two stories; this allows students to compare and contrast the experiences of two different Americans who are from the same general region, in addition to comparing the experiences of Americans from different regions. Many different factors can be used to identify and define "regions" within a country. It is very important to explain to readers that regions are created by people to more easily define places that share similar characteristics but that, as human constructions, regions do not have clearly defined boundaries and that the actual geographic boundaries of a region are open to debate.

It is also important to let students know that, even though the material is organized geographically by region, the stories contained within each unit represent cultural patterns *found throughout the United States and not just in that particular region.* In fact, some cultural values are mentioned numerous times in stories throughout the book, allowing students to see that a particular cultural pattern is shared by a variety of U.S. Americans who live in different regions of the country. However, remind students that not all Americans uphold a particular cultural value, whether they are from the same geographic region or from different parts of the United States.

The 28 stories in this textbook were selected because they represent a *pattern* of cultural values found throughout the United States (see section Understanding U.S. American Values on pages xxii–xxiv for more information on the core values identified in this book). This means that, in general, U.S. Americans may tend to have the values illustrated by the stories in this book. However, it is important for you as the teacher to help your students understand that while these stories illustrate common cultural values, students may meet U.S. Americans who do not share one or more of these values. To do this, you may want to discuss the difference between generalizations and stereotypes—

noting that generalizations are about patterns found in a culture but they will not apply to everyone in that culture. Generalizations serve as guidelines only. Stereotypes, on the other hand, are statements often based on limited data that are applied to everyone from that culture. Please emphasize with your students how important it is to get to know each person and to understand his or her background, without applying stereotypes or cultural information that may not be true for that individual. Help your students recognize that all persons have been culturally conditioned to some extent and that their behaviors may reflect some of this cultural conditioning. Students will have the opportunity to explore the diversity in cultural values further through the Real Life Application activities (see pages xxi–xxii for a description of these activities).

In reading these personal stories, direct students to think about how the writers have been influenced by their cultural upbringing, with the majority of Americans having values that are tied to their heritages but also to living in this country, even if they were born in another country. Americans are an amalgamation of different cultural influences. In trying to understand Americans and what they value, it's important to understand the extent of cultural conditioning within U.S. American culture, especially given the diversity of the United States. So what are those patterns of cultural conditioning that make U.S. Americans "American"? This textbook is designed to help your students understand some of the patterns of that cultural conditioning, reflected through authentic American voices.

Within each unit and each story, the Presentation-Practice-Use approach is used. The Presentation occurs through the cultural notes, stories, comprehension questions, and vocabulary activities; the Practice occurs through the writing/speaking questions; and the Use occurs through the real life applications.

- Each story begins with **pre-reading activities,** including questions to focus the students on the personal story. Questions usually address the geographic location of the writer (to give students the context of location), as well as the cultural issues that will be raised in the story. A vocabulary prediction activity familiarizes students with a few key vocabulary words in the story and encourages them to predict the meaning of the words. (These words may not be common in other academic contexts, but they are important for understanding the story.) Students should look up actual definitions and write them in the book. As the teacher, you may even want to discuss a couple of these words further if you feel it would be helpful in increasing students' comprehension of the story. (Some of the stories have footnotes that you may need to explain to help your students understand the story more fully as they read it.)

- A **cultural note** introduces the student to the reading and to the underlying cultural value(s) addressed in the personal story. This cultural element is further elaborated later in the unit in a section called Culture

Application, which is designed to encourage students to think about what the cultural value means in terms of interacting with U.S. Americans and understanding U.S. American culture better.

- A **reading (story)** in authentic English is the featured highlight of each unit (most units contain two stories) and is the basis on which the other materials and activities for each unit are built. The stories vary in degree of difficulty, with a few of the easier ones toward the beginning of the text and the most complex story, both context-wise and vocabulary-wise, concluding the text in Unit 15. <u>Note</u>: Some readings can and do illustrate more than one cultural pattern. However, for the purposes of this text, just one or two cultural patterns are emphasized for each reading.

- **Cultural application** notes follow each story and briefly highlight what students should "take away" culturally from the story in regard to interacting successfully with U.S. Americans. <u>Note</u>: These application notes are broad generalizations so be sure to stress with students that they will not apply in all of their interactions with U.S. Americans. Additionally, these cultural applications aren't meant to imply that students need to use these to assimilate but are provided to help students understand U.S. American behavior better and to help them be more successful in their interactions.

- **Comprehension questions** (and, in some cases, also true/false questions) reinforce reading skills, including fact finding, synthesizing knowledge, and overall understanding of the reading passage.

- **Vocabulary exercises** are included to help students understand new vocabulary words in the story. These vocabulary words can be pre-taught at the beginning of the story and then used as review after reading the story. These words were selected based on several factors, including frequency use in the text, consultation of high-intermediate/ advanced vocabulary lists, and actual experiences with students regarding problem words. Specifically, the pre-teaching contains words that may aid in understanding the reading but are not necessarily high-frequency words in academic text. The vocabulary activity following the reading, however, focuses on high-frequency words, more commonly used words, or commonly used words with not so commonly used definitions for those words. The entire vocabulary part is based on Celce-Murcia (1991)'s 3 C's approach to addressing vocabulary: (1) **conveying** meaning, which is done in the pre-teaching exercise; (2) **checking** understanding, which is done in the vocabulary exercises at the end of each story; and (3) **consolidation**, which involves students actually using the new vocabulary words. This is done by asking students to write original sentences at the end of each vocabulary exercise. This last part is very important since it forces students to do more than just memorize or understand definitions and, instead, facilitates students' actual usage of the vocabulary words. Teachers are also encouraged to develop other activities for their students to consolidate vocabulary usage, including writing stories, dialogues, and so on. These vocabulary words can also be used to reinforce spelling through spelling tests or spelling bees. Encourage students to keep a vocabulary notebook and list any new vocabulary learned through the stories.

- The combined **writing and speaking activities** focus on the cultural aspects of the story and allow students to reflect further on what they experience in U.S. American culture as well as from their own culture and cultural conditioning. These activities also provide an opportunity for students to practice what they will do in their conversations with U.S. Americans in the Real Life Applications that follow. Teachers are encouraged to use the questions for writing practice first for the following reason: speaking activities that include a preparation component "promote more successful student output" (Folse, 2006, p. 49). By having students think about the questions and write answers first, they are able to produce more complex language. That being said, it is not mandatory or desired for your students to always write their answers before discussing them in pairs or small groups. Depending on the needs of your students, they may not need such preparation before speaking but might benefit from discussing the questions first before responding in writing.

- The final activity for each authentic story is the **Real Life Application** in the community, which takes students from practicing in the classroom to using this information in the real world. Each Real Life Application includes a directed interaction with U.S. Americans in the community, often asking Americans questions similar to those the students practiced in class. (This is intentional so that, in most cases, students will have practiced the questions first in class before going to ask those questions to native English speakers.) Encourage students to write the responses from U.S. Americans they talk to and then to report back in class. These responses could possibly be written in a "culture journal" specific to this activity. Reporting on their interactions will promote further discussion in class and a deeper understanding of U.S. culture as students gain information and insights from these interactions. (Note that you will need to help provide suggestions as to how your students can connect with Americans in the community, such as through community clubs, sports clubs, church groups, or reading groups.) Other Real Life Applications for each story include opportunities for observation in the community, use of authentic materials in the community, or further research that will reinforce and expand students' cultural understanding. Some real life activities may seem similar from unit to unit, which is partly intentional so that students can become comfortable with engaging in those activities, some of which have slightly different foci, depending on the unit and cultural themes of the stories.

Engagement with U.S. Americans in the community is a vital part of this textbook in that it not only provides students with real life practice, but it gives students the opportunity to interact with U.S. Americans in meaningful ways in order to build relationships, practice their English, and gain deeper insights into U.S. American culture. Sharing and debriefing with your students regarding these Real Life Applications can become a rich part of the course. These Real Life Applications are a unique feature of this textbook .

- **End-of-Unit Activities** encourage students to think about the cultural insights they have gained through the stories and activities and to think in terms of how they will use this information in their daily interactions. One of those activities is to record their insights in a Notes chart found in the last unit of this textbook (see pages 202–10). It's very important that students complete this chart as they work through the textbook so that their cultural notes can easily be found in one location for the final reflection activities, which need to be completed in the concluding unit of the textbook.

- Add **listening activities** by reading the stories out loud instead of asking students to read them. Other activities can be added to enhance each chapter, such as focusing on key grammar elements that may emerge in the various stories or encouraging your students to role-play various situations found in the stories as a way for them to not only practice their English but to have them more fully experience the stories.

It is important to cover as many units, or even partial units, as possible in your course. We have found that students benefit from exposure to all of the units in this textbook. Working through these units will help your students develop a more comprehensive understanding of the deeper layers of U.S. American culture.

Understanding U.S. American Values

Many intercultural scholars have researched and written about cultural values in the United States. This textbook utilizes the work of Robert Kohls, who identified thirteen cultural values that summarized patterns found within U.S. American culture (see Table 1). The stories that appear in this textbook were selected to help illustrate these core values. Storti's work (2004) on American Values, *Americans at Work: A Guide to the Can-Do People*, was also consulted. You may want to reflect on how these values are, or are not, exhibited in the behaviors of the U.S. Americans whose stories appear in this book.

Some Values of U.S. Americans (Kohls, 2001, 2004)

1. **Personal Control over the Environment**: People can/should control nature, their own environment, and their own futures. *Result*: Energetic, goal-oriented society.

2. **Change/Mobility:** Change is good/positive; change represents progress, improvement, growth. New is better. *Result:* Transient society—geographically, economically, and socially.

3. **Control of Time:** Time is valuable and limited. *Result:* Efficiency and progress at the expense of relationships

4. **Equality/Egalitarianism:** All people have equal opportunities; basic worth is not assigned to individuals due to gender, birth, race, age, or status. *Result:* Status is not acknowledged.

5. **Individualism, Independence, and Privacy:** People are viewed as individuals (not group members) who have their own needs and who need time to be alone. The success of the individual is most important. *Result:* U.S. Americans may be viewed as self-centered, isolated, and lonely.

6. **Self-Help:** Americans take pride in own accomplishments. *Result:* Respect is given for achievements.

7. **Competition/Free Enterprise:** Competition brings out the best, and free enterprise produces the most progress. *Result:* Less emphasis on cooperation, except in some settings (i.e., work teams).

8. **Future-Oriented/Optimism:** Regardless of past or present, future will be better/happier. *Result:* Constantly looking ahead; little value on past or traditions.

9. **Action- and Work-Oriented:** Work is morally right; identity is defined by work. *Results:* More emphasis on "doing" than on "being." Time is wasted if nothing is accomplished or done.

10. **Informality:** Formality is a show of arrogance and superiority. *Result:* Casual attitudes between people; use of first names is common.

11. **Directness, Openness, Honesty:** Directness is usually not a sign of rudeness or disrespect but rather openness and efficiency. Americans may become annoyed when someone is not direct and may view indirectness as a form of dishonesty. *Result:* U.S. Americans tend to tell the truth and seemingly disregard a person's feelings without regard to someone else saving "face/honor." U.S. Americans don't want you to say anything just to please them.

12. **Practicality/Efficiency:** Most important consideration in decision-making. *Result:* Americans may place less emphasis on emotional or consensual decisions.

13. **Materialism:** Accumulation of material goods seen as rewards of hard work. *Result:* Americans are viewed as caring more for things than for people or relationships.

Kohls' (2001, 2004) thirteen values represent *patterns* found within U.S. American culture, but individuals may not necessarily fit those existing patterns. Thus, while the values highlighted in this textbook can be used as a guide for understanding behavior, it remains imperative for students to understand that not all U.S. Americans fit the patterns illustrated by the values identified by Kohls. It is also important to help your students understand that culture is much more complex than the values represented in this textbook—this is just a start in beginning to understand U.S. American culture and the behaviors students may encounter in daily interactions. It is also helpful to ask your students to reflect on the values found in other cultures (see Table 1) and to note how they differ from those in the U.S. Make sure students understand that values are not right or wrong, just different.

Table 1. Kohls' Values	
U.S. Majority Values	**Values of Other Cultures**
Personal Control over the Environment	Fate
Change	Tradition
Time and Its Control	Human Interaction
Equality	Hierarchy/Rank/Status
Individualism/Privacy	Group's Welfare
Self-Help	Birthright Inheritance
Competition	Cooperation
Future Orientation	Past Orientation
Action/Work Orientation	"Being" Orientation
Informality	Formality
Directness/Openness/Honesty	Indirectness/Ritual/"Face"
Practicality/Efficiency	Idealism
Materialism/Acquisitiveness	Spiritualism/Detachment

Understanding Theoretical Cultural Frameworks

Various theoretical cultural frameworks have been developed, such as ones by Geert Hofstede, with his focus on four dimensions of culture, or Edward Hall's work (1990) on aspects of cross-cultural communication. As Hofstede (1991) noted, "the main cultural differences among nations lie in values" (p. 236). Thus, understanding these values becomes crucial in understanding others. In teaching the deeper elements of U.S. American culture, it is helpful to understand the general concept of "culture" and the various cultural frameworks that shape an individual's values, beliefs, and behaviors.

Culture has been defined in a variety of ways, from "software of the mind" (Hofstede 1991) to a "blueprint for interactions" (Magala 2005) to "patterns, explicit and implicit, of and for behavior acquired . . . of human groups" (Kroeber & Kluckhorn, 1952, p. 181) to simply "the shared way of life of a group of people" (Berry, 2004, p. 167). Culture is an ever changing, complex phenomenon that shapes the lens through which individuals view the world around them and influences individuals' assumptions, attitudes, and behaviors. According to DeCapua and Wintergerst (2004), "the culture in which individuals are raised is the most important determinant of how they view and interpret the world" (p. 13).

What is important to remember in relation to this textbook is that culture goes beyond what is known as *objective* culture (history, literature, music and so on) to include *subjective* culture (Triandis, 1994), which comprises the less tangible aspects of culture such as beliefs, values, attitudes, and meanings. These aspects ultimately influence and condition the behaviors that are experienced in daily interactions. Thus, a visual depiction of a definition of culture is known as the iceberg concept of culture (see Figure 1). In this visual depiction,

Figure 1. The Iceberg Concept of Culture

Surface Culture
Above sea level
Emotional load: relatively low

food ▪ dress ▪ music ▪
visual arts ▪ drama ▪ crafts
dance ▪ literature ▪ language
celebrations ▪ games

Deep Culture

Unspoken Rules
Partially below sea level
Emotional load: very high

courtesy ▪ contextual conversational patterns ▪ concept of time
personal space ▪ rules of conduct ▪ facial expressions
nonverbal communication ▪ body language ▪ touching ▪ eye contact
patterns of handling emotions ▪ notions of modesty ▪ concept of beauty
courtship practices ▪ relationships to animals ▪ notions of leadership

Unconscious Rules
Completely below sea level
Emotional load: intense

tempo of work ▪ concepts of food ▪ ideals of childrearing
theory of disease ▪ social interaction rate ▪ nature of friendships
tone of voice ▪ attitudes toward elders ▪ concept of cleanliness
notions of adolescence ▪ patterns of group decision-making
definition of insanity ▪ preference for competition or cooperation
tolerance of physical pain ▪ concept of "self" ▪ concept of past and future
definition of obscenity ▪ attitudes toward dependents ▪ problem-solving
roles in relation to age, sex, class, occupation, kinship, and so forth

Indiana Department of Education ▪ Office of English Language Learning & Migrant Education ▪ www.doe.in.gov/englishlanguagelearning

culture includes not only what is concrete and visible in a culture but also what is not visible. This textbook focuses on the less visible aspects of culture, namely underlying cultural values that influence behavior. Values here are defined as shared assumptions about what is important to a group of people, which "fundamentally influence the behavior of individuals" in that group (DeCapua & Wintergerst, 2004, p. 18).

There are three levels of human behavior—the personal, cultural, and universal levels. Behavior at the personal level is what makes us all unique as individuals. Behavior at the

Figure 2. Behavior Pyramid

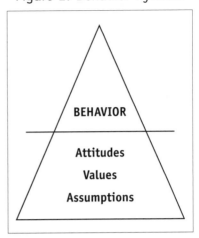

cultural level is how we as individuals have been culturally conditioned by the group(s) to which we belong to behave in socially acceptable ways in that particular cultural group. Behavior at the universal level encompasses behaviors that all humans may have in common. This textbook focuses on understanding behavior that is culturally conditioned. As illustrated by this behavior pyramid (see Figure 2), if we want to understand behavior in other cultures (which is the visible part of the interaction), it is important to understand the assumptions, values, and attitudes that lie beneath that behavior. This textbook thus helps students explore some underlying cultural values, as a tool for understanding the behaviors that they encounter in their daily interactions.

Developing Intercultural Competence

Ultimately, what does this understanding of cultural values lead to? By understanding values in another culture, students can enhance their own intercultural competence—their effective and appropriate behavior and communication with others. What do we mean by intercultural competence? The intercultural competence framework in Figure 3 (Deardorff, 2006, 2009) was used as one of the theoretical frameworks in developing this textbook.

In this model, there are three main components of intercultural competence (attitudes, knowledge, and skills) that lead to the internal and external outcomes that enable us to be more successful in our intercultural interactions. A key aspect of the knowledge component is culture-specific knowledge—which is where the underlying cultural values play an essential role. It's not enough to just know the language or customs or facts about another culture; rather, these values influence the behavior we encounter. Another key aspect in the knowledge component of intercultural competence is "cultural self-awareness," which has also guided the development of this textbook. The activities associated with each story intentionally help students reflect on their own cultures in an effort to help them gain a greater cultural self-awareness and to

Figure 3. Intercultural Competence Model

Process Model of Intercultural Competence (Deardorff, 2006, 2009):

Individual

Attitudes:
Respect (valuing other cultures);
Openness (withholding judgment);
Curiosity & discovery (tolerating ambiguity)

Knowledge & Comprehension:
Cultural self-awareness, deep cultural knowledge, sociolinguistic awareness

SKILLS: To listen, observe & evaluate; To analyze, interpret & relate

Process Orientation

Desired External Outcome:
Effective and appropriate communication & behavior in an intercultural situation

Desired Internal Outcome:
Informed Frame of Reference Shift (adaptability, flexibility, ethnorelative view, empathy)

Interaction

Notes:

• Begin with attitudes; Move from individual level (attitudes) to interaction level (outcomes)

• Degree of intercultural competence depends on acquired degree of attitudes, knowledge/comprehension, and skills

From "The Identification and Assessment of Intercultural Competence as a Student Outcome of Internationalization at Institutions of Higher Education in the United States" by Dr. K. Deardorff in *Journal of Studies in International Education*, Fall 2006, 10, p. 241–266 and in *The SAGE Handbook of Intercultural Competence*, 2009 (Thousand Oaks: Sage).

process the cultural learning that they are experiencing in their daily living experience in this country.

Crucial to intercultural competence development is reflection. A starting point for understanding any culture is with one's own culture. Thus, teachers are strongly encouraged to use this text as a reflective tool for their students in order to enhance students' intercultural competence development. To facilitate such reflection, space has been provided at the end of each unit to allow students to reflect on the readings, on what these readings helped them understand about their own cultures, and on the implications for understanding behaviors. Journaling is also an excellent way to engage in this reflective learning, and teachers are encouraged to ask their students to keep a journal throughout the use of this text and beyond regarding insights they are gaining into U.S. American culture. Be sure to ask students to reflect on more than *what* they are learning, to understanding *why* what they are learning is important and which actions/behaviors they will use as a result. You may choose to collect these journals periodically or on a regular basis to gain insight into what your students are learning and what questions they may still have about cultural learning. You can also use these reflective writings to help guide your students toward a greater degree of intercultural competence.

An Intercultural Tool

As a way to help students develop their intercultural competence, teachers may want to teach students to use this tool in their interactions with U.S. Americans and with others. This tool specifically addresses some of the key aspects of intercultural competence, including observation, coupled with skills to analyze and evaluate. The OSEE Tool (Deardorff & Deardorff, 2000) allows students to challenge their own cultural assumptions in order to move beyond initial reactions to better understanding behaviors they encounter in daily interactions. Initially developed in 2000 and based on the scientific method, it has been used in cross-cultural training programs and courses.

O— Observe what is happening.

S — State objectively what is happening.

E — Explore different explanations for what is happening.

E — Evaluate which explanation is the most likely one.

—(Deardorff & Deardorff, 2000)

OSEE starts with the basics of observation and listening, of really being aware of what is occurring in intercultural situations. As noted in the intercultural competence model discussed here, this is an essential skill and a key starting point. The next step is to state as objectively as possible what is happening. This is much more difficult than it sounds, and there are a variety of activities that can be used to help students practice the development of objective statements, including viewing brief film clips and writing about them. The next step, that of exploring different explanations, addresses the need to see from others' perspectives. It also allows one to begin to move beyond initial assumptions that may have inadvertently been made. Different explanations could include personal and cultural explanations, the latter of which necessitates the need to know culture-specific information, including knowledge of underlying cultural values. The last step—that of evaluation—is the most difficult since it is often challenging to know which explanation is the most likely one for the situation that is occurring. There are a number of different ways to evaluate the likely explanations, including collecting further information through conversations with others and by asking questions. When these steps are followed, one is able to view behaviors more objectively, thus achieving a measure of intercultural competence.

Exposing students to the OSEE Tool can aid them in developing intercultural competence and will hopefully result in students beginning to move beyond cultural assumptions to realizing a key lesson to cross-cultural understanding: Most people do behave rationally; you just have to discover their rationale (Storti, 1994). The OSEE Tool helps students begin to understand the rationales behind the behaviors they encounter in intercultural situations, thus increasing their intercultural competence. As your students read these stories, encourage them to apply the OSEE Tool when possible and, especially, during their Real Life Application activities and daily interactions with U.S. Americans.

Note: If you are interested in learning more about cultural theories and how they manifest themselves in one's teaching practice, several highly recommended references are listed on page xxx.

Getting Started

In introducing this textbook in your course, we recommend that you start by asking the students to read and discuss the To the Students section. This will provide students with an overview of the textbook, including a rationale for why and how to use these stories as a tool for understanding deeper U.S. American culture and why it is important to explore underlying cultural values as a means for understanding behavior. During this discussion, it will be helpful for students to discuss their own definitions of culture and the differences between generalizations and stereotypes. You can then state how important it is to see these stories as illustrative of cultural patterns (not specific to a geographic area within the U.S.), which can guide them to a deeper and more holistic cultural understanding but will not necessarily explain all the behaviors they may encounter on a daily basis. Remind students that they will meet U.S. Americans who do not fit within the cultural patterns discussed in this textbook. You may also want to introduce the OSEE Tool to your students and ask them to practice with this tool in class by showing them photos of

U.S. Americans or video clips of TV shows and asking them to apply the OSEE Tool. You could also discuss critical cultural incidents and ask them to apply the OSEE Tool through activities such as small group discussion or written essays.

We hope that this background information has been helpful in preparing you to use this textbook in your classroom and in teaching the deeper levels of culture. The goal in teaching culture is not to make our students into U.S. Americans but to help them understand U.S. Americans better. As DeCapua and Wintergerst (2004) have noted, "The role of teachers is to help learners become aware of the role of culture in forming people's interpretation of self in relation to others and the world around them" (p. 28). We encourage you to be creative in adapting these materials or using these stories and activities as a springboard for your own teaching as you guide your students toward greater cultural awareness, both of themselves and of others. Suggestions are welcome and should be directed to the University of Michigan Press (esladmin@umich.edu). Ultimately, we hope that this textbook will give your students a deeper, more holistic understanding of U.S. culture.

References

Berry, J.W. (2004). Fundamental psychological processes in intercultural relations. In *Handbook of intercultural training,* (eds.) D. Landis, J.M. Bennett, & M.J. Bennett. Thousand Oaks, CA: Sage.

Celce-Murcia, M. (1991). *Teaching English as a second or foreign language.* Boston: Heinle & Heinle.

Deardorff, D.K. (2006). The identification and assessment of intercultural competence as a student outcome of internationalization at institutions of higher education in the United States. *Journal of Studies in International Education*, 10(3), 241–266.

Deardorff, D.K. (2009). *The SAGE handbook of intercultural competence.* Thousand Oaks, CA: Sage

Deardorff, D.K., & Deardorff, D.L. (2000). *Diversity awareness and training: Tools for cultural awareness.* Presentation made at North Carolina State University, Raleigh.

DeCapua, A. , & Wintergerst, A.C. (2004). *Crossing cultures in the language classroom.* Ann Arbor: University of Michigan Press.

Folse, K. S. (2006). *The art of teaching speaking.* Ann Arbor: University of Michigan Press.

Hall, E.T., & Hall, M.R. (1990). *Understanding cultural differences.* Yarmouth, ME: Intercultural Press.

Hofstede, G. (1991). *Cultures and organizations: Software of the mind.* Berkshire, U.K.: McGraw-Hill.

Kohls, R. (2001). *Survival kit for overseas living.* Boston: Nicholas Bredey.

Kohls, R. (2004). *Values Americans live by.* San Francisco: Robert Kohls.

Kroeber, A.K. , & Kluckhorn, C. (1952). *Culture: A critical review of concepts and definitions.* Cambridge, MA: Peabody Museum.

Magala, S. (2005). *Cross-cultural competence.* New York: Routledge.

Storti, C. (2004). *Americans at work: A guide to the can-do people.* Yarmouth, ME: Intercultural Press.

Storti , C. (1994). *Cross-cultural dialogues.* Yarmouth, ME: Intercultural Press.

Triandis, H. (1994). *Culture and social behavior.* New York: McGraw-Hill.

Overview of Diversity in the United States

Part 1

▼ Pre-Reading Activities

Discuss these questions in pairs or small groups.

1. What do you know about the United States and its people? Talk in general about the people and the culture.

2. What are the backgrounds of the people who live in the U.S.?

3. How diverse do you think the U.S. is? What languages are spoken in the U.S.?

4. What is a typical American like? The typical American family?

▼ Vocabulary Prediction

Predict the meaning of these vocabulary words found in the story before reading the story. The word appears in a sentence or phrase from the story. After you have predicted the meaning, then look up the word in a dictionary and write the definition.

1. **immigrants**—*The United States is a land of immigrants.*

   Prediction: Immigrants means _____

   Definition: _____

2. **minorities**— . . . *with minorities projected to comprise 33 percent of the overall population.*

   Prediction: Minorities means _____

   Definition: _____

3. **indigenous**—*There are more than 300 languages spoken in the United States (162 indigenous languages and 149 immigrant languages) . . .*

   Prediction: Indigenous means _____

   Definition: _____

4. **refugees**—*With large numbers of refugees from more than 30 countries . . .*

   Prediction: Refugees means _____

   Definition: _____

5. **distinctiveness**— *. . . where the many different cultures are able to maintain their distinctiveness.*

   Prediction: Distinctiveness means _____

   Definition: _____

Think about these vocabulary words. What do you think this story will be about?

_____

Reading: Diversity in the United States

The United States is a land of immigrants. People from all over the world live in the United States, with minorities projected to comprise 33 percent of the overall population by 2020.[1] There are more than 300 languages spoken in the United States (162 indigenous and 149 immigrant languages) with the most common languages being English (more than 80 percent) and Spanish (more than 11 percent), and Chinese being the third-most spoken language at home.[2] The largest minority in the U.S. is the Spanish-speaking minority, followed by African Americans. States with the fastest-growing Spanish-speaking populations are Nevada, Washington, Oregon, Massachusetts, Virginia, North Carolina, and Florida.[3] With large numbers of refugees from more than 30 countries, the largest groups of refugees have come from the former Soviet Union, Vietnam, and the former Yugoslavia.[4] New York City, Los Angeles, and Chicago are home to the most number of refugees. States with the highest immigrant populations are California, New York, Texas, and Florida. With people from so many cultures, the United States is even a more diverse country now than it was in the early 20th century. The idea of a "melting pot" that was common in the 20th century no longer describes U.S. American culture. Today, it is more like a "salad bowl" or a "stew," where the many different cultures are able to maintain their distinctiveness, while at the same time embracing some common cultural values. This diversity means that U.S. American culture changes quickly—new words are added and traditions are introduced. So, what are some of those common cultural values, despite the diversity? This book will help you explore some of those common values shared by many Americans.

---

[1] U.S. Census data, "U.S. Interim Projections by Age, Sex, Race," 2004. For more detail, see www.census.gov/ipc/www.usinterimproj.
[2] See www.vistawide.com/languages/us_languages2.htm.
[3] Pew Hispanic Center, 2005. See also www.ushcc.com/res-statistics.html.
[4] From Migration Information Source, 2007, www.migrationinformation.org.

▶ Comprehension Questions

Discuss these questions about the reading in pairs or small groups.

1. What is the largest minority in the United States?

2. Which area(s) are growing the fastest in minority groups?

3. Why is a "salad bowl" or "stew" used to describe the U.S. now?

4. Why and how is U.S. American culture changing?

5. What was the most interesting point for you in this reading?

Cultural Application

This textbook will introduce you to some of the things that are important to U.S. Americans from many parts of the United States. You will read brief personal stories from a wide variety of U.S. Americans including African Americans, Hispanic Americans, Asian Americans, an Arab American, and some Native Americans. Through their own stories and in their own words, you will have the chance to learn more about what helps to make U.S. Americans *American*. Note: The authentic stories represent *patterns* found throughout U.S. American culture. Please remember that you will meet U.S. Americans who do not fit these cultural patterns.

▶ Vocabulary Exercise

These words appeared in the reading. This activity helps you see how well you understood the vocabulary words. Circle the best answer that most closely matches the meaning of the word. If there are any you don't know, add them to your vocabulary notebook.

1. **cultures**

   With people from so many cultures . . .

   cultures means
   a. economic groups
   b. societies
   c. clubs
   d. groups that share basic values and behaviors

2. **describes**

   The idea of a "melting pot" . . . no longer describes American culture.

   describes means
   a. misrepresents
   b. writes
   c. represents
   d. draws

3. **maintain**

   . . . where the many different cultures are able to maintain their distinctiveness.

   maintain means
   a. neglect
   b. continue
   c. discontinue
   d. deny

4. **diversity**

   This diversity means that U.S. American culture . . .

   diversity means

   a. not different

   b. variety

   c. sameness

   d. likeness

5. **traditions**

   . . . U.S. American culture changes quickly—new words are added and traditions are introduced.

   traditions means

   a. customs

   b. dress

   c. stories

   d. food

▉ Vocabulary Usage

Now, it's your turn to practice using these vocabulary words. Choose at least two vocabulary words, and write your own sentences using these new words in your vocabulary notebook.

▉ Writing/Speaking Practice

Choose one or more of these topics to write about or discuss in pairs or small groups.

1. Describe the different groups of people in the country you were born in—are there immigrants? What countries or cultures are people from in your country? What languages are spoken in your country?

2. Describe someone you know who is from a different culture and who lives in the United States. Where is that person from? What language(s) does that person speak? What are some of the customs in that culture?

3. Compare the diversity of the population in the United States with diversity in the country where you were born.

4. What can we learn from people from different cultures?

5. Describe some friends, neighbors, or co-workers you have from the U.S. What are their cultural backgrounds?

6. How do you think diversity changes U.S. American culture?

▶ Real Life Application: Interacting with U.S. Americans

Activity 1

Find at least one U.S. American, and ask that person these questions. Then report back to the class.

1. Tell me about your family. Where is your family originally from? What can you tell me about the cultural or ethnic history of your family?

2. What is your opinion about diversity in the United States?

3. How has the area in which you live changed in recent years? How have the recent changes to the population affected you personally?

Activity 2

Look through U.S. magazines, and cut out pictures of Americans. Try to find pictures of many different Americans. Make a collage of these pictures. What do these pictures reveal about Americans?

Activity 3

Find out how many different countries and languages are represented at the local school near you. To do this, you will need to contact the school office. Your teacher can help you do this.

Part 2

▼ Pre-Reading Activities

Discuss these questions in pairs or small groups.

1. Find Minneapolis on the map. What do you know about Minnesota?

2. Why do people move to the United States?

3. What do you think when you hear the word *home*?

▼ Vocabulary Prediction

Predict the meaning of these vocabulary words found in the story before you read the story. The word appears in a sentence or phrase from the story. After you have predicted the meaning, then look up the word in a dictionary and write the definition.

1. **agricultural**—*I came as an agricultural exchange student.*

   Prediction: **Agricultural** means _____

   Definition: _____

2. **fit in**—*I feel that I fit in with the culture . . .*

   Prediction: **Fit in** means _____

   Definition: _____

3. **figured**—*I figured that I live here . . .*

   Prediction: **Figured** means _____

   Definition: _____

Based on these vocabulary words, what do you think this story will be about?

_____

Cultural Note: Home

Throughout this book, stories will be introduced by a Cultural Note such as this one. The word *home* has many different meanings to U.S. Americans. To some it means their actual house; to others it means their hometown. A story of one immigrant's journey to home and how he came to understand and adapt to differences follows. This textbook will help you understand cultural differences of the people in this country as you make a new home in the United States. Gaining a better understanding of different types of U.S. Americans will improve your daily interactions.

Tonu's Story—St. Paul, Minnesota

I came to the United States from Estonia at the age of 23. I came as an agricultural exchange student. On the second day after my arrival to Minneapolis, I was picked up by my host farmer and driven to my placement farm in northern Minnesota. I am now 39 years old, married and have two children. I became a U.S. citizen. It took me 14 years to become comfortable with the idea that I would call the United States my home.

It has been a long road. Over time, I have come to associate more and more with other Americans. When I first came, most of my friends were other international students. I feel that I fit in with the culture, I enjoy my work, and I love my family. I enjoy working on my house, going on bike rides along the Mississippi River and traveling to various places in the U.S. It feels like home now. I figured that I live here, work here, raise children here, and own a house here, so I might as well be able to vote.

There are things that I miss about Estonia of course: Favorite foods, closeness of my parents and high school friends, and long summer days. There are things that I would miss about the United States if I wasn't living here anymore: Things like crossing the Mississippi River on my way to work or the greetings of our cat when I arrive home. In fourteen years, I have created memories in the United States that keep me here. I was married here and both of my children were born here. Almost all of my working life, I have spent in the United States. These memories are dear to me. Over time, things that struck me as strange don't seem so strange any more. Thus I have changed in the time that I have been in the United States. This is my home now.

◤ Comprehension Questions

Discuss this story in pairs or small groups.

1. Where is Tonu from originally?

2. How long did he live in the United States before becoming a citizen?

3. What does he miss about his home country?

4. What would he miss about the United States?

5. Where is home for Tonu and why?

6. What was the most interesting point for you in this reading?

Cultural Application

You will find that U.S. Americans may not always live in the same place where they grew up, although quite a few do. However, it is common to find U.S. Americans who have lived quite a few different places or whose family originally came from another country. Think about what this means in terms of **home** for U.S. Americans. Why do U.S. Americans live in several different locations during their lifetime? U.S. culture is considered to be more mobile—with citizens moving for education, for jobs, or for retirement. How is this similar or different from your experience? What does this mean when you meet U.S. Americans who have lived in several different locations? Do you think U.S. Americans may make friends quickly and have more acquaintances than close friends? (Note: You'll read about another person's perceptions of home in Unit 5, and you'll read more about American ideas on friendship in Unit 13.)

▶ Vocabulary Exercise

These words appeared in the reading. This activity helps you see how well you understood the vocabulary words. Circle the answer that most closely matches the meaning of the word. If there are any words you don't know, add them to your vocabulary notebook.

1. **associate**

   I have come to associate more and more with other Americans.

   associate means
   a. disconnect
   b. not like
   c. love
   d. connect

2. **various**

   . . . and traveling to various places in the U.S.

   various means
   a. same
   b. interesting
   c. nearby
   d. different

3. **created**

   I have created memories in the United States . . .

   created means
   a. formed
   b. drawn
   c. cut
   d. recorded

4. **struck**

   Over time things that struck me as strange . . .

   struck means
   a. hit
   b. reached
   c. come
   d. impressed

▛ Vocabulary Usage

Now it's your turn to practice using these vocabulary words. Choose at least two vocabulary words, and write your own sentences using these new words in your vocabulary notebook.

▛ Writing/Speaking Practice

Choose one or more of these topics to write about or discuss in pairs or small groups.

1. Describe your move to the United States. When did you come? How long have you been here?

2. What are some things you miss about the place where you were born?

3. What are some things you enjoy here in the United States?

4. Describe home. Where is home for you?

5. What are some ways you can connect with Americans?

▛ Real Life Application: Interacting with U.S. Americans

Activity 1

Ask a few U.S. Americans these questions, and then report back to your class.

1. Where is your hometown? Where is your home? If your hometown and home are different, please explain.

2. How many places have you lived? How often have you moved?

3. What does home mean to you? What would miss you about home?

4. What are some things you really enjoy doing?

5. What advice can you give about how to connect with U.S. Americans?

Activity 2

Look in the newspaper or look online to find some activities that you would enjoy doing in the area where you live; activities could include going to a movie, a concert, bowling, or shopping. Try to do one activity in the next week (if possible, try to connect with at least one U.S. American through that activity) and then tell your classmates about what you did.

Part 3

▼ Pre-Reading Activities

Discuss these questions in pairs or small groups.

1. Find Puerto Rico on a map. What do you know about Puerto Rico?

2. Have you ever helped a stranger? If so, how?

3. What is your opinion about smiling at others?

4. When you were growing up, what were you taught about smiling?

5. Do you think U.S. Americans smile a lot? What does smiling mean?

▼ Vocabulary Prediction

Predict the meaning of these vocabulary words found in the story before you read the story. The word is provided in a sentence or phrase from the story. After you have predicted the meaning, then look up the word in a dictionary and write the definition.

1. **unleash—** . . . *how the smile of a stranger could unleash so many joyful emotions within me.*

    Prediction: Unleash means _____

    Definition: _____

2. **sincere—** . . . *a smile that was sincere and came straight from the heart.*

    Prediction: Sincere means _____

    Definition: _____

3. **effect—** . . . *that it has as much of an effect on others as it has on yourself.*

    Prediction: Effect means _____

    Definition: _____

Based on these vocabulary words, what do you think this story will be about?

_____

Cultural Note: Smiling

Some U.S. Americans smile a lot. Smiles can have different meanings, so it is important not to confuse the meaning of a smile. It does not mean the same thing in the United States as it means in other countries, and it may not mean the same thing from two different U.S. Americans. One U.S. American shares her thoughts about smiling in the next story.

Viviana's Story—Ponce, Puerto Rico

The day I came to understand the power of a smile I was 12, and it completely changed my perspective of life. I was walking towards the car after I had forgotten my beach towel. Across the parking lot there was a grandfather playing with his granddaughter. When I walked past them the grandfather looked me in the eyes and smiled. My eyes filled with tears of joy.

At first, it was difficult to understand how the smile of a stranger could unleash so many joyful emotions within me. I realized it was a smile filled with love and happiness, a smile that was sincere and came straight from the heart. I then decided that what I once learned from the grandfather at the beach I would apply in my personal life. Day in and day out, I tried to seal all of my actions with a smile. As people would smile back at me, I realized that the most important thing about smiling is that it has as much of an effect on others as it has on yourself. Every time I exchange a smile with someone I feel like something is being said but most important, a smile without reason can inspire individuals to live in happiness, at least for a day.

▼ Comprehension Questions

Discuss these questions about the reading in pairs or small groups.

1. What made Viviana happy?

2. What did Viviana learn from the grandfather?

3. How do people respond to Viviana when she smiles?

4. What does Viviana believe about smiling?

5. What was the most interesting point for you in this reading?

Cultural Application

You may find that U.S. Americans smile at you more than you are used to. When U.S. Americans smile at you, what does this mean? Generally, this simply means they are being friendly to you. How should you respond? Smile back at them. If someone from the opposite sex smiles at you, generally this also means that he or she is just being friendly. Some people think that Americans are "fake" because they smile a lot. Again, understand that this is actually their way of being friendly. (For a note about the friendliness versus friendship, see Unit 13.) In regard to other nonverbal types of communication, please remember that it is often very important to make direct eye contact with Americans when talking with them and not to look away or down. Making eye contact shows respect in U.S. American culture.

▶ Vocabulary Exercise

These words appeared in the reading. This activity helps you see how well you understood the vocabulary words. Circle the answer that most closely matches the meaning of the word. If there are any you don't know, add them to your vocabulary notebook.

1. **perspective**

   . . . and it completely changed the perspective of my life.

   perspective means
   a. view
   b. feelings
   c. attitude
   d. opinions

2. **emotions**

   . . . how the smile of a stranger could unleash so many joyful emotions within me.

   emotions means
   a. concerns
   b. feelings
   c. attitudes
   d. thoughts

3. **realized**

   I realized it was a smile filled with love and happiness . . .

   realized means
   a. misunderstood
   b. appreciated
   c. understood
   d. did not know

4. apply

. . . I would apply in my personal life.

apply means

a. give

b. forget

c. ignore

d. use

5. inspire

. . . a smile without reason can inspire individuals to live in happiness, at least for a day.

inspire means

a. motivate

b. to not care

c. to not affect anyone

d. unmotivate

Vocabulary Usage

Now, it's your turn to practice using these vocabulary words. Choose at least two vocabulary words, and write your own sentences using these new words in your vocabulary notebook.

▼ Writing/Speaking Practice

Choose one or more of these topics to write about or discuss in pairs or small groups.

1. What is your opinion about smiling? Do you think it is important to smile? When do you smile? What makes you smile? What does it mean when you smile? Do you smile at people you don't know? Why or why not?

2. Describe an experience of when a U.S. American smiled at you. Did you know this person? How did the smile make you feel?

3. What brings you joy?

4. How can you help make someone happy?

▼ Real Life Application: Interacting with U.S. Americans

Activity 1

Ask a few U.S. Americans these questions, and then report back to your class.

1. How much do you smile every day (a little, some, a lot)? What makes you smile? Do you smile at people you don't know?

2. Have you ever helped a stranger? If so, how?

3. Do you think it's important to smile? Why or why not?

Activity 2

Now it's time to practice your observation skills. Go to a mall, a restaurant, or some other public place and observe U.S. Americans smiling. When do they seem to smile? Who are they smiling at? Do you know why they might be smiling? Do they smile at strangers? What non-verbal communication do you see? Write your observations, and then share those in class.

▶ End-of-Unit Activities

List at least one new cultural insight you gained from this unit that helps you understand U.S. American culture a little better.

Based on the information in this unit, write one or two things that you will do or that you want to remember that will improve your interactions with U.S. Americans.

Turn to the Notes section at the end of this textbook (page 203), and complete the section related to Unit 1.

UNIT 2

Underlying Cultural Values in the United States

Part 1

Pre-Reading Activities

Discuss these questions in pairs or small groups.

1. What do you think is important to U.S. Americans?
2. What makes U.S. Americans "American"?
3. How do you describe U.S. American culture?
4. What do you think some of the differences are between U.S. American culture and your culture?

Vocabulary Prediction

Predict the meaning of these vocabulary words found in the story before you read the story. The word is provided in a sentence or phrase from the story. After you have predicted the meaning, then look up the word in a dictionary and write the definition.

1. **materialism**—*Values such as individualism, freedom, and materialism have helped shape American culture.*

   Prediction: Materialism means ______________________________

   Definition: ______________________________

2. prosperity—*They came in search of freedom and prosperity . . .*

Prediction: Prosperity means _____

Definition: _____

3. persecution—*Some came to escape religious persecution . . .*

Prediction: Persecution means _____

Definition: _____

Based on these vocabulary words, what do you think this reading will be about?

_____

Reading: U.S. Cultural Values

Within the diversity of the United States, there is something that is also uniquely American. What makes U.S. American culture "American" within the diversity of the U.S.? There are some underlying cultural values within the U.S. and while not all Americans believe in them, those values have shaped U.S. American culture. Values such as individualism, freedom, and materialism have helped shape American culture. These values were influenced by the history of the United States. Do you know why Europeans come to the North American continent so long ago? They came in search of freedom and prosperity and a chance for a better life. Some came to escape religious persecution in their home countries. Some religious beliefs have actually helped shape U.S. American culture too—like the "Protestant work ethic" of belief in hard work. These values help condition U.S. Americans to behave and communicate in ways that make them "American."

▼ Comprehension Questions

Discuss this reading in pairs or small groups.

1. What are some key values that are important to many Americans?

2. What has influenced these values?

3. What values are similar to values in your culture? Which ones are different?

4. What was the most interesting point for you in this reading?

Cultural Application

By understanding the cultural values in different cultures, you will be better able to understand why people behave the way they do. In that way, you can avoid making the wrong assumptions about people. When you encounter behavior that is different from what you expect, stop and ask yourself: What could be some reasons for why this person is behaving this way? Consider that culture may be one of those reasons. See page xxviii for an intercultural tool to use to move beyond making assumptions.

▼ Vocabulary Exercise

These words appeared in the reading. This activity helps you see how well you understood the vocabulary words. Circle the answer that most closely matches the meaning of the word. If there are any you don't know, add them to your vocabulary notebook.

1. **uniquely**

   Within the diversity of the United States, there is something that is also uniquely American.

   uniquely means

   a. ordinarily

   b. typically

   c. commonly

   d. distinctively

2. **underlying**

   There are some underlying cultural values within the U.S. . . .

   underlying means

   a. to be the foundation of

   b. to be at the top of

   c. not forming a basis for

   d. non-supportive

3. **values**

   There are some underlying cultural values within the U.S. . . .

   values means

   a. beliefs

   b. benefits

   c. amounts

   d. principles

4. **condition**

   These values help condition U.S. Americans to behave and communicate in ways that make them "American."

   condition means

   a. influence

   b. state of health

   c. comfortable

   d. control

▶ Vocabulary Usage

Now, it's your turn to practice using these vocabulary words. Choose at least two vocabulary words, and write your own sentences using these new words in your vocabulary notebook.

▶ Writing/Speaking Practice

Choose one or more of these topics to write about or discuss in pairs or small groups.

1. What values are important in the culture you grew up in? Which values are important to you personally?

2. What two or three values do you think are most important to U.S. Americans?

3. Compare and contrast your cultural values with those in the United States.

▶ Real Life Application: Interacting with U.S. Americans

Activity 1

Ask a few U.S. Americans these questions, and then report back to your class.

1. What is important to you as an American?

2. What values are important in American culture?

3. What makes Americans "American"?

4. What do you think is important to know in order to better understand Americans and American culture?

Activity 2

Watch an American film like "Working Girl," and try to identify underlying cultural values that can be found in U.S. American culture.

Activity 3

Get some U.S. magazines and find ads that illustrate some values that are important to U.S. Americans. You can make a collage and share this with the class. You could also make a collage with photos that are important for illustrating values important to you.

Cultural Application

Culture is sometimes defined as an iceberg (see page xxv). At the tip of the iceberg are the parts of culture that are easy to see and experience, such as language, food, music, arts, dress, and so on. However, there is much more that is necessary in understanding culture—how people think, what they believe in, what influences their behaviors and attitudes. This is the part of culture that is more difficult to see. This book, through the voices of real U.S. American citizens, will help you gain a deeper understanding of U.S. American culture—the part that is often not seen or understood. By reading these short personal stories, you will embark on a journey through U.S. American culture and gain a deeper understanding of Americans—enjoy!

Part 2

▶ Pre-Reading Activities

Discuss these questions in pairs or small groups.

1. Find Louisiana on a map. What do you know about Louisiana or "Cajuns"?

2. What is your opinion about freedom in the U.S.?

3. How is freedom thought about in your own culture?

4. What do you think the impact (the result) of "freedom" is on Americans and their culture?

▶ Vocabulary Prediction

Predict the meaning of these vocabulary words found in the story before you read the story. The word is provided in a sentence or phrase from the story. After you have predicted the meaning, then look up the word in a dictionary, and write the definition.

1. **embodied**— . . . *the one they think of as being embodied in the Declaration of Independence.* . . .

   Prediction: Embodied means _____

   Definition: _____

2. **forbearers**—*My forbearers were evicted at gunpoint from the original colony. . . .*

Prediction: Forbearers means _____

Definition: _____

3. **evicted**—*My forbearers were evicted at gunpoint from the original colony. . . .*

Prediction: Evicted means _____

Definition: _____

4. **assimilate**— *. . . even as they strive to assimilate.*

Prediction: Assimilate means _____

Definition: _____

5. **abridged**— *. . . and that if his freedom is abridged, mine may be next.*

Prediction: Abridged means _____

Definition: _____

Cultural Note: Freedom

U.S. Americans highly value personal freedom, and this is usually traced to the U.S. Constitution's Bill of Rights, which guarantees freedom of speech, among other freedoms. In the story that follows, you will read one American's thoughts about the importance of personal freedom. The story also includes examples of other U.S. American values that will be discussed in later stories—hard work, personal control over one's environment, and self-sufficiency and independence.

Matt's Story—Atlanta, Georgia

I believe in personal freedom. Most Americans believe in the general idea of freedom, the one they think of as being embodied in the Declaration of Independence and the Constitution's Bill of Rights—and so do I. But I believe the Founding Fathers sought freedom not just for a nation, but for each individual within that nation.

I come by this belief at least in part through my Cajun ancestry. My forbearers were evicted at gunpoint from their original colony in Nova Scotia by the British, and came to these shores determined that no one would ever displace them again. They founded a community in southeast Louisiana that was rich in culture and heritage, hardworking and self-sufficient, deeply spiritual and fiercely independent. In short, they were quintessentially[1] American.

From the Pilgrims onward, we Americans have been a feisty, strong-willed, nonconformist,[2] rebellious[3] lot. It's this attitude that makes . . . immigrants believe they deserve to hang on to at least some of their ancestral culture even as they strive to assimilate. It makes Americans fight in Iraq and Afghanistan and work to end slavery in the Sudan and disease caused by suffering in Kenya.

I believe that we do need some reasonable limits on personal freedom. But above all, I believe in and treasure the right to disagree, and in fighting for it even when it lets the most odious,[4] repugnant[5] views boil to the surface, like racism or homophobia[6] or flagburning. For I know that the fundamentalist's[7] freedom to speak and write and campaign is my freedom to do likewise, and that if his freedom is abridged, mine may be next.

---

[1] *quintessentially* means the most typical example, or totally.
[2] *nonconformist* means a person who does not accept the beliefs and customs of the majority.
[3] *rebellious* means to resist rules or control.
[4] *odious* means feelings of strong dislike.
[5] *repugnant* means offensive and disgusting.
[6] *homophobia* means fear of same-sex relationships.
[7] *fundamentalist* refers to someone with strong religious beliefs and principles.

▛ Comprehension Questions

Discuss these questions from the story in pairs or small groups.

1. Where are Matt's ancestors from originally?

2. How does Matt describe U.S. Americans (four words or phrases)?

3. What is the result of freedom in the U.S., according to Matt?

4. Why does Matt think freedom is so important and worth fighting for?

5. Why does Matt think it's OK for others to express their opinions, even though those opinions can hurt others?

6. What was the most interesting point for you in this reading?

▛ Reading Comprehension: True or False?

Read the sentences, and decide whether they are true or false based on the information in the story. Write T for true or F for false.

_____ 1. Matt's ancestors are from Canada.

_____ 2. Matt's ancestors moved to Mississippi.

_____ 3. Personal freedom and the freedom of speech come from the Declaration of Independence and the Bill of Rights.

_____ 4. Matt thinks that Americans should not be allowed to burn the U.S. flag.

Cultural Application

So, what does this cultural value of personal freedom mean? It means that you may find that U.S. Americans like to express what they believe and will sometimes do this through writing letters to the newspaper or to their government representatives. They may also express their opinions quite openly and may not like to be told what to do, say, or think. Many Americans will openly talk about U.S. politics, and it is generally considered appropriate to agree or disagree respectfully. They may also expect you to give your opinion on various issues, so try to be ready to do so.

⚑ Vocabulary Exercise

These words appeared in the reading. This activity helps you see how well you understood the vocabulary words. Circle the answer that most closely matches the meaning of the word. If there are any you don't know, add them to your vocabulary notebook.

1. **determined**

   . . . and came to these shores determined that no one would ever displace them again.

   determined means

   a. doubting

   b. hesitated

   c. not sure

   d. sure

2. **displace**

   . . . and came to these shores determined that no one would ever displace them again.

   displace means

   a. remove

   b. keep

   c. leave

   d. make them stay

3. **heritage**

   They founded a community in southeast Louisiana that was rich in culture and heritage . . .

   heritage means

   a. not from the past

   b. not inherited

   c. future

   d. from the past

4. **feisty**

   . . . we Americans have been a feisty, strong-willed, nonconformist, rebellious lot.

   feisty means

   a. calm
   b. obedient
   c. lively
   d. respectful

5. **hang on to**

   . . . immigrants believe they deserve to hang on to at least some of their ancestral culture . . .

   hang on to means

   a. stop
   b. discontinue
   c. continue
   d. let go of

6. **strive**

   . . . even as they strive to assimilate.

   strive means

   a. try
   b. ignore
   c. start
   d. to not attempt

Vocabulary Usage

Now, it's your turn to practice using these vocabulary words. Choose at least two vocabulary words, and write your own sentences using these new words in your vocabulary notebook.

▶ Writing/Speaking Practice

Choose one or more of these topics to write about or discuss in pairs or small groups.

1. Describe your understanding of freedom in U.S. American culture.

2. Describe the role of freedom in another culture. Do people express their opinions? If so, how and about what?

3. Compare and contrast freedom in another culture and in the U.S.

4. What is your opinion about the right to say what you want (freedom of speech)?

▶ Real Life Application: Interacting with U.S. Americans

Activity 1

Ask a few U.S. Americans these questions, and then report back to your class.

1. Tell me your opinion about the freedom of speech in the U.S.

2. How important do you think personal freedom is in the U.S.? How important is it to you?

3. Tell me four words or phrases that can be used to describe some Americans.

Activity 2

Find some letters to the editor in the local newspaper, and bring one or two examples to share with the class in which local citizens share their opinions on an issue. Consider writing your own Letter to the Editor.

◢ End-of-Unit Activities

List at least one new cultural insight you gained from this unit that helps you understand U.S. American culture a little better.

Based on the information in this unit, write at least one or two things that you will do or that you want to remember to improve your interactions with U.S. Americans.

Turn to the Notes section at the end of this textbook (page 203), and complete the section related to Unit 2.

UNIT 3

A Look at the Northeast

Part 1

Pre-Reading Activities

Discuss these questions in pairs or small groups.

1. Find Boston on the United States map. What state is it in? What other states are around this one? What do you know about Boston? Do you know anyone from there?

2. How do you celebrate birthdays? Is there one birthday that is more special?

3. What type of gifts do you usually receive on your birthday?

4. How do U.S. Americans celebrate birthdays?

5. How important is it to do things without anyone's help?

Vocabulary Prediction

Predict the meaning of these vocabulary words found in the story before you read the story. The word is provided in a sentence or phrase from the story. After you have predicted the meaning, then look up the word in a dictionary, and write the definition.

1. **certificate**—*He also gave me a certificate for a basic mechanics class through our local community college . . .*

   Prediction: Certificate means________________________________

   Definition: ______________________________________

2. mechanic— *. . . so that I would be able to change my own oil, change my own tire, and know if a mechanic was trying to rip me off. . . .*

Prediction: **Mechanic** means _____

Definition: _____

3. lasted— *. . . I still change my own tires, the car was great—it lasted all the way through college. . . .*

Prediction: **Lasted** means _____

Definition: _____

Based on these vocabulary words, what do you think this story will be about?

_____

Cultural Note: Independence, Materialism

Being independent in the U.S. means being able to do things without help. Having material goods is seen as a reward for working hard; this means that many U.S. Americans have a lot of material goods. In the next story, look for examples of both independence and materialism.

Kate's Story—Boston, Massachusetts

In our family, the 16th birthday was a big deal. You get to have a party and invite your friends. All the birthdays before 16 and after, birthday parties were just celebrated with only family at a restaurant of your choice and with a cake of your choice and, of course, presents. At 16, not only did I get a party, but it is also the age when I was able to get my driver's license. For my 16th birthday, I was given a string of pearls from my grandmother, Vavoa—we all got pearls at 16 in my family. I had my party—it was great, all my friends came and I served a 6-foot long submarine sandwich made on a 6-foot long roll served on a board. Then my Dad surprised me by giving me our old yellow 1970 Toyota Corolla that had more rust than body paint, and I loved it. He also gave me a certificate for a basic mechanics class through our local community college so that I would be able to change my own oil, change my own tire, and know if a mechanic was trying to rip me off by fixing things that really didn't need to be fixed on my car when it was broken. The class was great—I still change my own tires, the car was great—it lasted all the way through college, the pearls are still lovely—I will give them to my daughter when she turns 16 and the sandwich will go down in history as the coolest party munchies ever served at Brookline High School. I would say that is my favorite birthday memory.

▚ Comprehension Questions

Please discuss this story in pairs or small groups.

1. What gifts did Kate receive for her birthday?

2. How did she celebrate her 16th birthday?

3. How were birthdays usually celebrated in Kate's family?

4. What did Kate learn to do? Why was this important? What does this say about Americans being independent?

5. What was the most interesting point for you in this reading?

▚ Reading Comprehension: True or False?

Read the sentences, and decide whether they are true or false based on the information in the story. Write T for true or F for false.

_____ 1. Kate got a new car for her birthday.

_____ 2. Kate and her friends ate a huge sandwich at her party.

_____ 3. Kate's great aunt gave her a pearl necklace for her birthday.

_____ 4. Kate learned how to change the tires on her car.

_____ 5. Kate and her family celebrate birthdays with a big party every year.

Cultural Application

What do these cultural values of materialism and independence mean for you? The value of independence means that you may find U.S. Americans who are reluctant to ask for help and would prefer to do things on their own (although there are, of course, some examples of times when U.S. Americans may come together to help each other, especially in times of disasters). The value of materialism means that you may find U.S. Americans who have collected quite a lot of things in their homes and some who really enjoy shopping to purchase new items, including the latest fashions. Some Americans may have yard sales to get rid of things they don't want anymore or may simply take those items to a thrift store. You may also see Americans throwing away items that seem to be useful or good so they can buy new ones.

◢ Vocabulary Exercise

These words appeared in the reading. This activity helps you see how well you understood the vocabulary words. Circle the answer that most closely matches the meaning of the word. If there are any you don't know, add them to your vocabulary notebook.

1. **big deal**

    In our family, the 16th birthday was a big deal.

    big deal means
    a. special treat
    b. ordinary occasion
    c. everyday event
    d. important celebration

2. **rip me off**

    . . . and know if a mechanic was trying to rip me off . . .

    rip me off means
    a. cheat
    b. being honest
    c. be real
    d. tell the truth

3. **go down in history**

. . . I will give them to my daughter when she turns 16 and the sandwich will go down in history. . . .

go down in history means

a. will be forgiven

b. will be forgotten

c. will always be remembered

d. will never be recorded

4. **coolest**

. . . the sandwich will go down in history as the coolest party munchies ever served . . .

coolest means

a. without warmth

b. unenthusiastic

c. excellent

d. most unique

5. **munchies**

. . . the sandwich will go down in history as the coolest party munchies ever served . . .

munchies means

a. big meal

b. snacks

c. appetizers

d. feast

Vocabulary Usage

Now, it's your turn to practice using these vocabulary words. Choose at least two vocabulary words, and write your own sentences using these new words in your vocabulary notebook.

Writing/Speaking Practice

Choose one or more of these topics to write about or discuss in pairs or small groups.

1. Describe a special birthday memory you have.
2. Describe the best gift you ever received.
3. Discuss how people in another culture celebrate birthdays. Are some birthdays more special than others? Please explain.
4. What is your opinion of U.S. Americans being independent, and how is this similar or different from people in another country? Provide examples.
5. How important is it to have your own car in the U.S.? In another country? Explain.
6. Compare materialism in another country and in the U.S. How is it similar? What are the differences in materialism between these two countries?

Real Life Application: Interacting with U.S. Americans

Activity 1

Ask a few U.S. Americans these questions, and then report back to your class.

1. How are birthdays usually celebrated in your family?
2. What are some typical birthday gifts to give?
3. How important is it to have your own car? Tell me about your first car.
4. What do you think are some examples of individual Americans being independent?

Activity 2

Research examples of Americans being independent. Some ideas for how to research this are given.

1. Visit a local bookstore and find the "How to" section. Write down the names of some book titles you find there.

2. Find out what classes are being offered in your area that help Americans learn how to do a certain skill. You can look at classes offered through a local community college or university. Write down some examples.

Activity 3

Write some idioms and colloquialisms that you hear U.S. Americans say. Try to find out what they mean. You can listen for idioms on TV shows or find idiomatic expressions in newspaper articles.

Activity 4

Try to find a copy of the book called *Material World,* which has pictures of people from around the world with their possessions. (The local library may have a copy of this for you to borrow.) Look at the example for the U.S. as well as for another country in the book. Discuss these examples in class.

Part 2

▶ Pre-Reading Activities

Discuss these questions in pairs or small groups.

1. Find New York City on a map. What do you know about the city?

2. What is the hardest work you've ever done?

3. What kinds of jobs exist in the U.S. that involve hard work?

4. What do you think makes for a good worker?

▶ Vocabulary Prediction

Predict the meaning of these vocabulary words found in the story before you read the story. The word is provided in a sentence or phrase from the story. After you have predicted the meaning, then look up the word in a dictionary, and write out the definition.

1. **chambermaid**— *. . . but my grandma, Maminon, was a chambermaid at The Plaza. . . .*

   Prediction: Chambermaid means _____

   Definition: _____

2. **nobility**—*My grandmother taught us the nobility of hard, honest work.*

   Prediction: Nobility means _____

   Definition: _____

3. **dignity**—*I hold the value of the simple dignity of honest labor . . .*

   Prediction: Dignity means _____

   Definition: _____

Based on these vocabulary words, what do you think this story will be about?

_____

Cultural Note: Work Is Valued

U.S. Americans are generally considered to be hard-working and, in many cases, their identity is defined by the type of work they do. A story that is an example of a hard-working American follows.

Maria's Story—New York City, New York

I am Maria de los Angeles and I am a city child who never lived at The Plaza. I lived in an apartment in the Projects in Manhattan, but my grandma, Maminon, was a chambermaid at The Plaza and she was proud to work in such a grand place. She always called it The Hotel. She talked about the famous people who gave her extra tips because she did such a good job. Her gray eyes sparkled when she described the men's tuxedos and the women's beautiful jewels and fur wraps. I was so excited when Maminon told me that I was old enough to join her and my two older sisters on the visit to The Hotel during Easter vacation. We had the new spring coats and patent leather shoes and white gloves we bought for Easter. A handsome doorman opened the door for us. We went upstairs where we met the Housekeeper, a very important person, who offered us juice and cookies. The housekeeper said, "Your grandmother is the best worker on my floor. You must be very proud of her." We certainly were. My grandmother taught us the nobility of hard, honest work. She taught us the pride of accomplishment in a job well done. I hold the value of the simple dignity of honest labor as a core principle in how I live my life, encourage my children to live theirs and fight for the right of every hard-working person to earn a living that reflects that his/her work is valued.

▶ Comprehension Questions

Please discuss this story in pairs or small groups.

1. Where did Maria live as a little girl?

2. Where did Maria's grandmother work?

3. What did Maria do at Easter one year?

4. What did Maria buy?

5. What did the housekeeper give Maria?

6. What did Maria's grandmother teach her about work?

7. What was the most interesting point for you in this reading?

Cultural Application

What does it mean that Americans value work? It means that one of the first questions you get when you meet someone is, "What do you do?" The answer is quite important. U.S. Americans like to know about what kind of work you do. They also often expect others to work hard and to do a good job and to be successful in U.S. American society.

▶ Vocabulary Exercise

These words appeared in the reading. This activity helps you see how well you understood the vocabulary words. Circle the answer that most closely matches the meaning of the word. If there are any you don't know, add them to your vocabulary notebook.

1. **proud**

    . . . and she was proud to work in such a grand place.

    proud means
    a. satisfied
    b. sad
    c. disappointed
    d. bored

2. **sparkled**

    Her gray eyes sparkled when she described the men's tuxedos . . .

    sparkled means
    a. dulled
    b. watered
    c. closed
    d. twinkled

3. **accomplishment**

    She taught us the pride of accomplishment in a job well done.

    accomplishment means
    a. arrival
    b. achievement
    c. non-performance
    d. skill

4. **core**

I hold the value of the simple dignity of honest labor as a core principle in how I live my life. . . .

core means

a. main or central

b. small

c. outer

d. not important

5. **valued**

. . . and fight for the right of every hard-working person to earn a living that reflects that his/her work is valued.

valued means

a. useless

b. hopeless

c. appreciated

d. not important

◤ Vocabulary Usage

Now, it's your turn to practice using these vocabulary words. Choose at least two vocabulary words, and write your own sentences using these new words in your vocabulary notebook.

▼ Writing/Speaking Practice

Choose one or more of these topics to write about or discuss in pairs or small groups.

1. What was your first job?

2. Describe your current work. What do you do? How many hours do you work each week?

3. What is your dream job?

4. What are your beliefs about work?

5. What are some differences in work between another country and the U.S.?

▼ Real Life Application: Interacting with U.S. Americans

Activity 1

Ask a few U.S. Americans these questions, and then report back to your class.

1. What was your first job?

2. What is your current job, and how many hours do you work each week?

3. What advice can you give to someone about being successful at work?

Activity 2

Look in the Classifieds section of the newspaper or online, and find two or three examples of job positions that sound really good to you. Share those with your class.

End-of-Unit Activities

List at least one new cultural insight you gained from this unit that helps you understand U.S. American culture a little better.

Based on the information in this unit, write one or two things that you will do or that you want to remember that will improve your interactions with U.S. Americans.

Turn to the Notes section at the end of this textbook (page 204), and complete the section related to Unit 3.

A Look at Washington, DC

Part 1

▼ Pre-Reading Activities

Discuss these questions in pairs or small groups.

1. What do you know about Washington, DC?

2. What do you know about the social class system in the U.S.? What have you observed about rich and poor people in the U.S.?

3. What is your experience with a social class system?

▼ Vocabulary Prediction

Predict the meaning of these vocabulary words found in the story before you read the story. The word is provided in a sentence or phrase from the story. After you have predicted the meaning, then look up the word in a dictionary, and write the definition.

1. brilliant—*My father was a brilliant man. . . .*

   Prediction: Brilliant means _____

   Definition: _____

2. schisms—*My father was a brilliant man, caught in a black skin and all the schisms that permeated black life. . . .*

   Prediction: Schism means _____

   Definition: _____

3. permeated—*My father was a brilliant man, caught in a black skin and all the schisms that permeated black life . . .*

   Prediction: Permeated means _____

   Definition: _____

4. character—*It's not about the difficulty as much as it's about how you handle it that gives you character.*

   Prediction: Character means _____

   Definition: _____

Cultural Note: Equality

U.S. Americans generally believe that a person's basic worth does not depend on gender, birth, race, age, or status (due to name, money, or social class). Here is a story that is an example of that belief.

Lawrence's Story—Washington, DC

My father was a brilliant man, caught in a black skin and all the schisms that permeated black life in Washington, DC, in the 1950s and '60s. He worked as an attorney by day and delivered medication by night for Professional Pharmacy. He did this as a matter of course, to support his family. On weekends, I'd go along with him. We never said much but I'd like to think he enjoyed the company as much as I did. Some evenings, I'd share a problem I was having at school or around the neighborhood with him. He'd listen intently, asking a question or two until he'd heard it all. He'd say, "You know, everything will work out. There's nothing new under the sun . . . "

His clients loved him, mostly because he cared for them. He managed their adoptions, filed their taxes, helped them buy homes and occasionally got their errant[1] children out of jail. He was respected universally as far as I could see. He taught me that people can be noble and debased[2] no matter

---

[1] *errant* means behaving wrongly.
[2] *debased* means lower in character.

where they come from. That trouble comes to everyone, whatever his or her status. It's not about the difficulty as much as it's about how you handle it that gives you character. To that end, integrity comes from within the man and not what's in his pockets. If you treat people with respect and as equals, you will earn the same from them whether they follow your same beliefs or not. Class has nothing to do with money.

▼ Comprehension Questions

Discuss this story in pairs or small groups.

1. What did Lawrence's dad do for a living?

2. What would Lawrence do with his dad on the weekends?

3. What did Lawrence and his dad talk about?

4. What did Lawrence's dad teach him?

5. What was the most interesting point for you in this reading?

▼ Reading Comprehension: True or False?

Read the sentences, and decide whether they are true or false based on the information in the story. Write T for true or F for false.

_____ 1. Lawrence's dad was a lawyer.

_____ 2. Lawrence's dad worked two jobs.

_____ 3. Lawrence would go with his dad to work.

_____ 4. Lawrence and his dad would talk a lot together.

_____ 5. Lawrence's dad thinks that rich people should be treated differently.

Cultural Application: Equality

Equality is valued in the United States, meaning that all persons are viewed as being equal. In the U.S., family name or title may not be as valued as in other cultures and, in general, status is not acknowledged in the same ways in U.S. culture as in other cultures. And in the end, what's important is what kind of person you are and the work that you do. So, in the United States, you should not expect special treatment because of age, title, gender, or family name.

▼ Vocabulary Exercise

These words appeared in the reading. This activity helps you see how well you understood the vocabulary words. Circle the answer that most closely matches the meaning of the word. If there are any you don't know, add them to your vocabulary notebook.

1. **intently**

   He'd listen intently. . . .

   intently means
   a. with undivided attention
   b. half-way
   c. not concentrating
   d. not caring

2. **clients**

   His clients loved him. . . .

   clients means
   a. strangers
   b. neighbors
   c. citizens
   d. customers

3. **managed**

He managed their adoptions. . . .

managed means

a. did
b. directed
c. achieved
d. delayed

4. **occasionally**

. . . and occasionally got their errant children our of jail.

occasionally means

a. never
b. regularly
c. sometimes
d. often

5. **difficulty**

It's not about the difficulty as much as it's about how you handle it that gives you character.

difficulty means

a. predicament
b. to go smoothly
c. ease
d. problem

◤ Vocabulary Usage

Now, it's your turn to practice using these vocabulary words. Choose at least two vocabulary words, and write your own sentences using these new words in your vocabulary notebook.

▼ Writing/Speaking Practice

Choose one or more of these topics to write about or discuss in pairs or small groups.

1. What is something you learned from your family?

2. Describe the class system in another country.

3. What is your experience in the U.S. with the social class system—what have you observed?

4. Compare and contrast the social class system in the U.S. and in another country.

▼ Real Life Application: Interacting with U.S. Americans

Activity 1

Ask a few U.S. Americans these questions, and then report back to your class.

1. What do you think about the social class system in the U.S.? Is there a class system? If so, how do you describe it?

2. What social class would you say you are in—low, middle, or high? How do you know?

3. Do you have friends who are in other social classes? Please explain.

Activity 2

Volunteer a few hours (or more!) to work in a homeless shelter or soup kitchen in your community. Try to have some conversations with both other volunteers as well as with some of the persons who come to the shelter or soup kitchen. (Your teacher can help you find out more information about where to go to volunteer.) Afterward, write about your experience and observations.

Activity 3

Watch an American movie like "The Pursuit of Happyness"—what do you observe about social class?

Part 2

◢ Pre-Reading Activities

Discuss these questions in pairs or small groups.

1. Have you ever been to Washington, DC, or do you know someone who has been there?

2. Is it possible to have too much freedom?

3. How important is it to express your opinion?

4. What are your thoughts about communicating with others?

◢ Vocabulary Prediction

Predict the meaning of these vocabulary words found in the story before you read the story. The word is provided in a sentence or phrase from the story. After you have predicted the meaning, then look up the word in a dictionary, and write the definition.

1. career— . . . *have a career in technology.* . . .

    Prediction: Career means _____

    Definition: _____

    2. opposition—in *the U.S., a person can voice opposition.*

    Prediction: Opposition means _____

    Definition: _____

3. opinion— . . . *China has now relaxed its policies about expressing personal opinions.* . . .

    Prediction: Opinion means _____

    Definition: _____

4. express— . . . *anyone can express what they think.* . . .

    Prediction: Express means _____

    Definition: _____

Cultural Note: Communication/Freedom of Expression

In the United States, individuals have the freedom to express their opinions and beliefs. Communicating directly with words is very important, which may not be the case in other cultures. Here is a story from an immigrant's perspective about the freedom of communicating one's opinions and beliefs.

Julu's Story—Washington, DC

I came to the U.S. a number of years ago from China to go to school. Later, I married an American, have a career in technology and have now received my American citizenship. Being an American means I have more freedom now—for example, in the U.S., a person can voice opposition. (In China, we were always told not to discuss politics, especially if it was negative toward a policy or government official—even though China has now relaxed its policies about expressing personal opinions, life can be still be difficult.) At least here, anyone can express what they think in regards to the government, businesses, issues, . . . although political correctness hinders some in my opinion. Having said that, being an American also means to have to put up with others' opinions, politics and their influence, which in my opinion, is not always a good thing—I call it "too much freedom."

In my traditional way of thinking, America is a land for those who are willing to work hard, to succeed, and to make a better life. Being an American means putting up with everything to live a happy life here. Most of all, being an American means being with my family and loved ones. It also means having a place where my children can work hard towards their dreams. They will have opportunities to do whatever they desire or dream to do. The sky is the limit here.

▚ Comprehension Questions

Discuss this story in pairs or small groups.

1. Where is Julu originally from and why did she leave?

2. What does Julu do?

3. Does Julu have U.S. citizenship?

4. What does Julu like about living in the U.S.? What does she not like?

5. According to Julu, the U.S. is a land for those who . . . ?

6. What was the most interesting point for you in this reading?

▚ Reading Comprehension: True or False?

Read the sentences, and decide whether they are true or false based on the information in the story. Write T for true or F for false.

_____ 1. Julu is from the U.S.

_____ 2. Julu works in the technology field.

_____ 3. Julu is single.

_____ 4. Julu is a mother.

_____ 5. Julu thinks it is important to be able to express political opinions.

Cultural Application

Communicating one's opinions and beliefs is one aspect of freedom in the U.S. In the United States, it's often important to be very clear in your communication, to say what you mean, and to be direct in your words (but not too direct). For example, it's OK to say no to someone or to let others know you disagree. It's also OK to share your opinions and expect others to share opinions too. When communicating in the U.S., it's important to give details and to not assume that others know what you're talking about or that they share the same opinions as you.

◤ Vocabulary Exercise

These words appeared in the reading. This activity helps you see how well you understood the vocabulary words. Circle the answer that most closely matches the meaning of the word. If there are any you don't know, add them to your vocabulary notebook.

1. **negative**

   In China, we were always told not to discuss politics, especially if it was negative toward a policy or government official . . .

   negative means

   a. good
   b. problem
   c. bad
   d. nice

2. **voice**

   . . . a person can voice opposition.

   voice means

   a. sing
   b. say
   c. read
   d. know

3. **hinders**

   . . . although political correctness hinders some in my opinion.

   hinders means

   a. slows down
   b. stops
   c. helps
   d. speeds up

4. **relaxed**

. . . even though China has now relaxed its policies about expressing personal opinions . . .

relaxed means
a. increased
b. stopped
c. paused
d. eased

5. **put up with**

. . . being an American also means to have to put up with others' opinions . . .

put up with means
a. tolerate
b. accept
c. like
d. not like

▶ Vocabulary Usage

Now, it's your turn to practice using these vocabulary words. Choose at least two vocabulary words, and write your own sentences using these new words in your vocabulary notebook.

▶ Writing/Speaking Practice

Choose one or more of these topics to write about or discuss in pairs or small groups.

1. What do you think is the best way to communicate with others, especially if you disagree with them?

2. Discuss some social problems in another country and/or in the U.S. What are these problems? What is your opinion about these problems? What can be done about them?

3. One way to express your feelings and beliefs is through poetry. Share a poem you have written or read a favorite poem out loud to other students. If you haven't written a poem, you may want to try to write one now (your teacher can give you some examples).

▼ Real Life Application: Interacting with U.S. Americans

Activity 1

Ask a few U.S. Americans these questions, and then report back to your class.

1. What is your opinion about freedom of speech? Is it possible to have too much freedom?

2. What is a topic or policy you disagree with and why?

3. What is your opinion about "political correctness"?

4. How would you describe the U.S. American style of communication?

Activity 2

Read an essay or a poem by a U.S. American author that demonstrates his or her opinion about a particular topic or issue. (You may find such an essay in the newspaper under "Editorials" or in news magazines; you may also find essays or poems online.) Write or discuss your thoughts after reading these writings. Do you agree with the writer's opinion? Why or why not?

Activity 3

Find articles in the newspaper or magazines (or online) that are about some of the social problems in the U.S. Bring those articles to class to share, and be prepared to discuss your opinion about these problems.

Activity 4

Observe how Americans communicate with each other; this can be done by watching a TV show or movie. Do Americans tend to use a lot of emotion or a little bit? Do they tend to say things directly or indirectly? Do they tend to use their hands when they talk? What kind of facial expressions do they tend to make? Write your observations about patterns you are finding about how Americans communicate, and then write about how this compares with your own communication style. Think about what you can do to adapt your communication style when communicating with Americans.

Activity 5

Find out if there's a "poetry slam" in your area and, if so, try to attend. How do the people express themselves? What topics are addressed?

◤ End-of-Unit Activities

List at least one new cultural insight you gained from this unit that helps you understand U.S. American culture a little better.

Based on the information in this unit, write at least one or two things that you will do or that you want to remember to improve your interactions with U.S. Americans.

Turn to the Notes section at the end of this textbook (page 204), and complete the section related to Unit 4.

A Look at Appalachia

Part 1

◤ Pre-Reading Activities

Discuss these questions in pairs or small groups.

1. Find West Virginia on a map. What do you know about West Virginia?

2. In your experience, what do people do together as a community?

3. What do you think U.S. Americans do together as a community?

◤ Vocabulary Prediction

Predict the meaning of these vocabulary words found in the story before you read the story. The word is provided in a sentence or phrase from the story. After you have predicted the meaning, then look up the word in a dictionary, and write the definition.

1. **kettle**— . . . *our family made apple butter out under the trees in a large copper kettle.*

   Prediction: Kettle means _____

   Definition: _____

2. **peel**—*My mom would call all of the neighbor women the night before to cut and peel the apples. . . .*

   Prediction: Peel means _____

   Definition: _____

3. **grind**— . . . *while all the men would grind the apples for cider.*

   Prediction: Grind means _____

   Definition: _____

4. **barrels**—*The cider that was left over was stored in the basement in barrels. . . .*

   Prediction: Barrels mean _____

   Definition: _____

Cultural Note: Community

Over the past few decades in the United States, the idea of community has changed. With the increased mobility by individuals in the U.S.,[1] along with other changes, some people do not have a particularly strong sense of belonging to their communities, especially in large, urban areas. U.S. Americans have become increasingly disconnected from families, friends, and neighbors since the 1970s, based on a study conducted by Harvard researcher Robert Putnam (2000).[2] Here is a story about community in years past.

---

[1] In 2009 and 2010, nearly 38 million people one year and older changed residences in the U.S. within the past year, with nearly 30 percent of that group moving to a different county in the same state or moving to a different state (U.S. Census Bureau, 2011).
[2] *Bowling Alone: The Collapse and Revival of American Community* by Robert D. Putnam, New York: Simon & Schuster.

Helen's Story—Franklin, West Virginia

In the fall of every year, our family made apple butter out under the trees in a large copper kettle. My mom would call all of the neighbor women the night before to cut and peel the apples while all the men would grind the apples for cider. The next afternoon we put the apples in the large copper kettle along with the cider, sugar, cinnamon and small amount of vinegar and let it boil for 3-1/2 hours. It had to be stirred all the time so all the young folks did that while the men sat around the fire, drinking cider and telling tales of long ago. When the apple butter was done and pulled away from the fire, my mom came out with her hot homemade bread and we all sampled the apple butter. It was stored in jars for the winter. My four brothers and I took it in our lunchbox every day to school for lunch. The cider that was left over was stored in the basement in barrels and when the neighbors stopped by on winter evenings, we served them hot cider and homemade donuts.

Comprehension Questions

Discuss this story in pairs or small groups.

1. What did Helen's family do every fall?
2. Who would help Helen's family with this activity?
3. How would Helen's family make apple butter?
4. How many brothers did Helen have?
5. What did Helen eat for lunch every day?
6. What would Helen's family do with the leftover cider?
7. What was the most interesting point for you in this reading?

Cultural Application

Cultures change. In U.S. American culture, community is something that has changed over time. Years ago, communities would be made up of neighbors who knew each other, often quite well, and who would engage in activities together. Today people in the same community may not know each other well and may not engage in activities together. In today's world, community exists in different forms, such as through online social networking sites (Facebook or LinkedIn, for example). You may want to consider joining a social networking site, if you are not already part of one and if you have the means to do so. Groups in your local community, such as church groups, book clubs, and sports teams, are also a way to be part of a community. If you're not already part of one of those groups, consider joining one.

▶ Vocabulary Exercise

These words appeared in the reading. This activity helps you see how well you understood the vocabulary words. Circle the answer that most closely matches the meaning of the word. If there are any you don't know, add them to your vocabulary notebook.

1. **stirred**

   It had to be stirred all the time. . . .

   stirred means
   a. not moving
   b. cooked
   c. moved
   d. remained still

2. **sampled**

   . . . my mom came out with her hot homemade bread and we all sampled the apple butter.

   sampled means
   a. didn't taste
   b. tasted
   c. ate all
   d. ate part

3. **stored**

It was stored in jars for the winter.

stored means

a. wasted

b. shopped

c. collected

d. kept

4. **homemade**

. . . we served them hot cider and homemade donuts.

homemade means

a. made by factory

b. store bought

c. made at home

d. made overseas

Vocabulary Usage

Now, it's your turn to practice using these vocabulary words. Choose at least two vocabulary words, and write your own sentences using these new words in your vocabulary notebook.

Writing/Speaking Practice

Choose one or more of these topics to write about or discuss in pairs or small groups.

1. Describe something you have done together with people from the community or neighborhood where you live now.

2. What is community like in another culture?

3. What are some of the differences and similarities between community in the U.S. and in another country?

▶ Real Life Application: Interacting with U.S. Americans

Activity 1

Ask a few U.S. Americans these questions, and then report back to your class.

1. How important is community to you?

2. What do you do together with people in your community? Describe a community or group you belong to.

3. How has community changed in the last ten years in the U.S.?

Activity 2

Look in the newspaper (or online), and find examples of community activities. Then try to attend one.

Part 2

▶ Pre-Reading Activities

Discuss these questions in pairs or small groups.

1. What do you think it would be like to grow up in a small mountain town?

2. Do you know anyone who grew up in the mountains?

3. What state or region are you from originally? How do you feel about that area?

4. When you think about the future, what emotions do you feel (for example, are you happy, worried, hopeful, discouraged, etc)?

▼ Vocabulary Prediction

Predict the meaning of these vocabulary words found in the story before you read the story. The word is provided in a sentence or phrase from the story. After you have predicted the meaning, then look up the word in a dictionary, and write the definition.

1. **winding**—*I believe in the winding roads. . . .*

   Prediction: **Winding** means _____

   Definition: _____

2. **hollows**—*I believe in the winding roads and the deep hollows.*

   Prediction: **Hollows** mean _____

   Definition: _____

3. **academic**—*I believe in the great academic institutions of this state. . . .*

   Prediction: **Academic** means _____

   Definition: _____

Cultural Note: Optimism

Optimism and hope in a better future have been a general belief in U.S. American culture. (Consider Barack Obama's 2008 campaign motto, "Yes, We Can!") Here is a story about one American's hope for the future as well as her love for her home state.

Megan's Story—Huntington, West Virginia

I believe in the state of West Virginia. I believe in the mist over the mountains in the morning when the sun rises, and in the evening when it sinks into the western rose colored sky. I believe in the valleys low and the mountains high, and the rivers that have run through them for ages. I believe in the winding roads and the deep hollows. I believe in the mild summers and the sun shining so brightly upon us all. I believe in autumn that brings us many colors. I believe in the oranges, golds, and reds of a West Virginia fall. I believe in cold breezes that bring snow, which is so pure and so beautiful. I believe in spring where everything is in bloom. The grass is greener, the skies are bluer and the air is still crisp. I believe in the beauty of the Mountain State.[1] I believe in the families of West Virginia. Homes large and small, apartments and houses, spread throughout the state. I believe in the warmth of community, the love of family, and the nurturing relationships built in these small mountain towns. I believe in coal miners, stay-at-home moms, bankers, steelworkers, teachers and the working class of West Virginia. I believe in the dreams of prosperity[2] and the future of the state. I believe that there is so much more in the future of West Virginia. I believe in the great academic institutions of this state where the future leadership of this state is built daily. I believe that we are not rednecks or hillbillies,[3] but we are people who love one another and love this state. I believe in West Virginia, the mountains, the valleys, the streams, but most importantly I believe in the people of West Virginia.

[1] *Mountain State* is the nickname for West Virginia.
[2] *prosperity* means success.
[3] *hillbilly* refers to a person from a remote mountain area or "backwoods."

◤ Comprehension Questions

Discuss this story in pairs or small groups.

1. What does Megan like about West Virginia?

2. What is the nickname for West Virginia?

3. Where do many families live in West Virginia?

4. What kind of jobs do people in West Virginia have?

5. What does Megan believe is the future of West Virginia?

6. What was the most interesting point for you in this reading?

Cultural Application

One result of U.S. Americans' focus on optimism and hope for the future is that Americans are often looking ahead to what will or could happen, sometimes giving little value to the past or even lessons learned from history. In other cultures, the past may be greatly valued, but in the U.S., there's a tendency to think that "what's in the past is in the past—let's move on." This may mean that U.S. Americans focus on positive aspects, no matter the situation. If you find yourself making lots of negative comments or thinking negative thoughts, you may want to consider making more positive comments instead. Ask yourself: What is something good in this situation? It is important to sound positive. Try not to say *that won't work;* instead say, *here's how we can make this work.* Try not to suggest giving up, and be especially careful when complaining or making excuses.

◤ Vocabulary Exercise

These words appeared in the reading. This activity helps you see how well you understood the vocabulary words. Circle the answer that most closely matches the meaning of the word. If there are any you don't know, add them to your vocabulary notebook.

1. **beauty**

   I believe in the beauty of the Mountain State.

   beauty means
   a. ugly
   b. handsome
   c. plain
   d. lovely

2. **spread**

   Homes large and small, apartments, and houses, spread throughout the state.

   spread means
   a. together
   b. stretched
   c. unrolled
   d. unfolded

3. **warmth**

   I believe in the warmth of community, the love of families. . . .

   warmth means
   a. glowing
   b. coldness
   c. unfriendliness
   d. friendliness

4. **nurturing**

   . . . and the nurturing relationships built in these small mountain towns.

   nurturing means

   a. cold

   b. not supportive

   c. caring

   d. uncaring

Vocabulary Usage

Now, it's your turn to practice using these vocabulary words. Choose at least two vocabulary words, and write your own sentences using these new words in your vocabulary notebook.

Writing/Speaking Practice

Choose one or more of these topics to write about or discuss in pairs or small groups.

1. Describe a special location in another place or country.
2. What is the most beautiful place you've been?
3. What are your hopes for the future?

▼ Real Life Application: Interacting with U.S. Americans

Activity 1

Ask a few U.S. Americans these questions, and then report back to your class.

1. What is your favorite state in the U.S.?

2. What is the most beautiful place you've been?

3. How long have you lived in this state and what are your thoughts about living here?

4. What do you feel about your future? What are your hopes for the future?

Activity 2

Research more information about a U.S. state in which you would like to live or visit. Write to the Chamber of Commerce of a city in that state and request tourist information. Prepare a poster about that state and share it in your class.

▛ End-of-Unit Activities

List at least one new cultural insight you gained from this unit that helps you understand U.S. American culture a little better.

Based on the information in this unit, write one or two things that you will do or that you want to remember to improve your interactions with U.S. Americans.

Turn to the Notes section at the end of this textbook (page 205), and complete the section related to Unit 5.

A Look at the South

Part 1

▼ Pre-Reading Activities

Discuss these questions in pairs or small groups.

1. Find Virginia on the map. What do you know about Virginia?

2. How do you help people in your community?

3. What do you know about Americans' faith beliefs? The religions in the U.S.?

▼ Vocabulary Prediction

Predict the meaning of these vocabulary words found in the story before you read the story. The word is provided in a sentence or phrase from the story. After you have predicted the meaning, then look up the word in a dictionary, and write the definition.

1. **pharmaceutical**—*My father worked . . . at a pharmaceutical company for forty years.*

   Prediction: Pharmaceutical means _____

   Definition: _____

2. **clerk**—*My father worked as a chemical clerk. . . .*

   Prediction: Clerk means _____

   Definition: _____

3. pastoral ministry—*God answered by prayer by introducing me to a handsome young man studying for the pastoral ministry. . . .*

Prediction: **Pastoral ministry** means _____

Definition: _____

Cultural Note: Religion, Future-Oriented

There are many different religions in the U.S., including Christianity, Judaism, and Islam. Here is a story that gives an example of a Christian woman's faith, her desire to help other people, and her thoughts about her future.

Kay's Story—Harrisonburg, Virginia

I was born in the beautiful Shenandoah Valley of Virginia, surrounded by majestic mountains and peaceful hills. My father worked as a chemical clerk at a pharmaceutical company for forty years. My mother was a homemaker and an excellent seamstress who made all of our clothing just by looking at pictures. My younger sister, brother, and I grew up in a Christian home with very loving parents. My growing up years were spent helping my parents in the garden, with home chores, going to school, going to church, and all of us working together to help people in our community. These experiences nurtured my goal to someday serve God by helping people in their journey of life. God answered my prayer by introducing me to a handsome young man studying for the pastoral ministry who soon became my husband. God gave us the privilege of serving 37 years in the pastoral ministry in churches from the East Coast of America to the West Coast—11 different churches. Throughout these years, I have been able to serve by my husband's side—together helping people in their journey of life.

▼ Comprehension Questions

Discuss this story in pairs or small groups.

1. Where was Kay born?

2. What did Kay's parents do?

3. What did Kay do when she was growing up?

4. What was Kay's goal in life?

5. What kind of man did she marry? (What was his job?)

6. What was the most interesting point for you in this reading?

▼ Reading Comprehension: True or False?

Read the sentences, and decide whether they are true or false based on the information in the story. Write T for true or F for false.

_____ 1. Kay was born in the city.

_____ 2. Kay had two brothers.

_____ 3. Kay's mother made clothes.

_____ 4. Kay and her husband worked at 11 different churches.

_____ 5. Kay and her husband lived on the East Coast.

Cultural Application

While many in the United States do not belong to a religious group, there are others that do. For example, a portion of the southern United States is sometimes called "the Bible Belt" because more people may belong to churches in that region. Be sure to be aware of the religious beliefs of U.S. Americans in your community, and how their beliefs may impact your interactions (for example, some people may not believe in drinking alcoholic beverages for religious reasons, or they may go to church on Sunday mornings and so are not available to do an activity with you at that time). You may also encounter those who want you to change the way you believe, to convert you to their religion. When asked about your beliefs, you can respond with "that's a private matter that I don't wish to discuss" if you really don't want to discuss it with the person who asked you. Religious beliefs can indeed greatly impact what people believe, their future goals, and how they respond to life's circumstances.

◤ Vocabulary Exercise

These words appeared in the reading. This activity helps you see how well you understood the vocabulary words. Circle the answer that most closely matches the meaning of the word. If there are any you don't know, add them to your vocabulary notebook.

1. **majestic**

   . . . surrounded by majestic mountains. . . .

   majestic means
   a. ordinary
   b. magnificent
   c. simple
   d. average

2. handsome

God answered my prayer by introducing me to a handsome young man. . . .

handsome means

a. ugly

b. pleasant

c. good-looking

d. unattractive

3. experiences

These experiences nurtured my goal to someday serve God by helping people. . . .

experiences mean

a. trips

b. work

c. events in one's life

d. vacations in one's life

4. privilege

God gave us the privilege of serving. . . .

privilege means

a. restriction

b. opportunity

c. advantage

d. disadvantage

▛ Vocabulary Usage

Now, it's your turn to practice using these vocabulary words. Choose at least two vocabulary words, and write your own sentences using these new words in your vocabulary notebook.

▛ Writing/Speaking Practice

Choose one or more of these topics to write about or discuss in pairs or small groups.

1. Describe the place where you were born. What did it look like?

2. What did you do when you were growing up?

3. What are your goals in life—what do you hope to do? Is it common to discuss such goals, based on your experience of where you grew up?

4. What do you believe in? Explain some of your faith/religious practices, if you have some and if you feel comfortable talking about them.

▛ Real Life Application: Interacting with U.S. Americans

Activity 1

Ask a few U.S. Americans these questions, and then report back to your class.

1. Where were you born? Describe this place.

2. What are your goals in life?

3. Do you have any religious or spiritual beliefs? If so, what are some of those (if you feel comfortable discussing them . . .)?

Activity 2

Consider visiting a place of worship in your community to observe what happens and who attends. The phone book lists places of worship under Churches, or you could talk with your teacher about a place you can go. Be sure to find out the day and time of the religious service, and what kind of dress/behavior is appropriate. You can do this by making a phone call to that place of worship before you visit. After your visit, write about your experience and bring what you have written to class.

Activity 3

Visit your local library or bookstore (or look online) to find books about various religions. Read at least one of those books and then write a report about what beliefs are important in that religion. Share your report with your class.

Part 2

▼ Pre-Reading Activities

Discuss these questions in pairs or small groups.

1. Find North Carolina on a map. What do you know about North Carolina?

2. How are persons from different races or religions treated in another culture with which you're familiar?

3. Have you ever experienced any negative behavior toward you based on your race, culture, or religion?

4. How important is it to learn and to gain knowledge?

▼ Vocabulary Prediction

Predict the meaning of these vocabulary words found in the story before you read the story. The word is provided in a sentence or phrase from the story. After you have predicted the meaning, then look up the word in a dictionary, and write the definition.

1. segregation—*I was raised as a black, Baptist girl in a society that denies its prejudice, and underlying segregation. . . .*

   Prediction: Segregation means _____

   Definition: _____

2. posterity—*I believe that individuals of all nations through labor and posterity can one day cause great changes in the world.*

   Prediction: Posterity means _____

   Definition: _____

3. responsibility—*I think that it is every person's responsibility to seek knowledge. . . .*

   Prediction: Responsibility means _____

   Definition: _____

> ## Cultural Note: Individualism, Equality
>
> Here is a story about a Muslim woman's faith beliefs, the equality of all, and the importance of individuals learning on their own so that they can be successful.

Kim's Story—Durham, North Carolina

I was raised as a black, Baptist girl in a society that denies its prejudice, and underlying segregation, but I choose to go beyond the boundaries that were imposed on me, and grew into an African American Muslim woman, who is a former Army specialist, a mother of three with a (family) culture that spans from African American, White, Mexican and Middle Eastern (Egypt). I believe in multiculturalism, where each person can retain his/her own culture while being a positive and successful influence to this society. I believe that individuals of all nations through labor and posterity can one day cause great changes in the world. That is, if we stop trying to make all men alike (believe, speak and think the same). All men are equal, but we are not all alike, and that is what makes us thrive and prosper, and grow and gain knowledge.

Growing up, I had the privilege of being in a family that taught me that color did not define who you were or what you could do—not so much in words, but in actions. I remember going camping, which where I came from, was unheard of for black kids to do. The kids in my neighborhood thought that we were rich kids, because of the things that we did. If a black person was sleeping outside, it was because they had no other choice, not for pleasure. My parents raised my sister and me to think for ourselves, and set no limits on what we could do. I think that is why I am always seeking knowledge, and open to new things in my life. I see everyone with the potential to do and be the best that they can be if we set no limits or boundaries in their lives.

I believe that we are all responsible for the knowledge that we gain. When I started reading about Islam, I realized that it was the true "for me" so without regard to what my family might think, I knew that it was the right thing—they realized that I was doing the right thing for me, and that I had not stopped believing in GOD, it was the way I worshipped that had changed. Now, after working at two jobs that were uncomfortable about my beliefs and me wearing a Hijab (head scarf), I have come to a place where I can be productive in my faith and in my workplace. I work at a university in their Islamic Studies Center, where I am the only Muslim on staff, and where I have the opportunity daily to be an example of what I believe. Each day I continue to grow, and gain knowledge, I think that it is every person's responsibility to seek knowledge, no matter if it is through books, other people or experiences and then apply that knowledge so that we grow as a people. Never stop learning, never give up on yourself or others.

▼ Comprehension Questions

Discuss this story in pairs or small groups.

1. Describe Kim.

2. What was Kim's religion when she was a child?

3. What is Kim's religion now?

4. Where are Kim's family members from?

5. Where did Kim used to work? What does she do now?

6. What does Kim believe?

7. What was the most interesting point for you in this reading?

Cultural Application

Education (and gaining knowledge as an individual) is an important value in U.S. American culture. Education is seen as a way to achieve equality within American society. This means that it is important to seek out ways to learn in the U.S.—workplaces may offer various trainings for employees and many colleges, for example, have continuing education programs that offer reasonably priced courses for adults to take, including courses in learning other languages, "how-to" courses, and literature courses. There are also certificate programs in which participants can earn certificates for learning about a particular area or topic. Individuals can also learn on their own by reading books or through online courses and resources. "Lifelong learning" is important in the U.S.—so keep learning!

Vocabulary Exercise

These words appeared in the reading. This activity helps you see how well you understood the vocabulary words. Circle the answer that most closely matches the meaning of the word. If there are any you don't know, add them to your vocabulary notebook.

1. **denies**

   I was raised as a black, Baptist girl in a society that denies its prejudice. . . .

   denies means

   a. confirms
   b. refuses to acknowledge
   c. affirms
   d. ignores

2. **prejudice**

   I was raised as a black, Baptist girl in a society that denies its prejudice. . . .

   prejudice means

   a. judgment made without adequate knowledge
   b. acceptance
   c. emotion
   d. tolerance

3. **boundaries**

   . . . but I choose to go beyond the boundaries that were imposed on me. . . .

   boundaries means

   a. no limits

   b. borderless

   c. limits

   d. no barriers

4. **retain**

   I believe in multiculturalism, where each person can retain his/her own culture. . . .

   retain means

   a. let go of

   b. continue to keep

   c. drop

   d. use

5. **thrive**

   . . . and that is what makes us thrive and prosper. . . .

   thrive means

   a. succeed

   b. fail

   c. get smaller

   d. try

Vocabulary Usage

Now, it's your turn to practice using these vocabulary words. Choose at least two vocabulary words, and write your own sentences using these new words in your vocabulary notebook.

▶ Writing/Speaking Practice

Choose one or more of these topics to write about or discuss in pairs or small groups.

1 *All men are equal, but we are not all alike.* What is your response to this sentence?

2. How do you view equality? How do you view multiculturalism?

3. Describe a time when you went beyond the boundaries.

4. Who or what has helped make a difference or bring about change—in a life, at work, or in the world?

5. What is your opinion about learning knowledge?

6. Do you think it is possible to retain one's own culture while living in the U.S.? Please explain. How can one adapt to life in the U.S. while still keeping one's own culture?

▶ Real Life Application: Interacting with U.S. Americans

Activity 1

Ask a few U.S. Americans these questions, and then report back to your class.

1. What is your opinion about equality in the U.S.?

2. Have you ever experienced any prejudice?

3. Do you believe it is possible for immigrants to retain their own culture while succeeding in the U.S.? Please explain.

4. What are some ways you learn new things? Have you ever taken a continuing education course or training at work? If so, what was your experience like?

Activity 2

Go to a mall, restaurant, park, or other public space and observe how people are treated. Do you notice any differences in how people from different races are treated? List your thoughts and observations and share those in class.

Activity 3

Find a course catalog (online or in hard-copy form) from a local college or community college, ideally one near you. Find out what courses are offered through the college's continuing education program (not all colleges offer such a program), and choose one that would be of personal interest to you. Share this with your class.

▼ End-of-Unit Activities

List at least one new cultural insight you gained from this unit that helps you understand U.S. American culture a little better.

Based on the information in this unit, write at least one or two things that you will do or that you want to remember to improve your interactions with U.S. Americans.

Turn to the Notes section at the end of this textbook (page 205), and complete the section related to Unit 6.

UNIT 7

A Look at the Deep South

Part 1

Pre-Reading Activities

Discuss these questions in pairs or small groups.

1. Find Alabama on the U.S. map. Have you been to Alabama, or do you know someone who has been there? What have you heard or read about Alabama?

2. What was life like for you growing up?

3. What lessons did your family teach you?

Vocabulary Prediction

Predict the meaning of these vocabulary words found in the story before you read the story. The word is provided in a sentence or phrase from the story. After you have predicted the meaning, then look up the word in a dictionary, and write the definition.

1. **impressed upon**—*My father impressed upon me. . . .*

   Prediction: Impressed upon means ______________________________

   Definition: ______________________________

2. **relish**— . . . *because the live stock, particularly cows, would relish the peels.*

   Prediction: Relish means ______________________________

   Definition: ______________________________

3. work ethic— . . . *a work ethic that is sadly often missing in America today.*

Prediction: Work ethic means _____

Definition: _____

Cultural Note: Work Is Valued, Efficiency/Practicality

Here is a story that discusses one American's experience with work in the United States. U.S. Americans are generally concerned about practicality and efficiency, of making the most of what they have, including time. Notice the example in the second paragraph that demonstrates practicality.

Becky's Story—Pike Road, Alabama

I grew up in a small farming community in South Alabama, the youngest of 5 children to older parents. (My father was almost 52 when I was born.) We all had to work in the fields and share chores of every day living. My father impressed upon me this lesson, "Any job that is worth doing at all is worth doing right"—a work ethic that is sadly often missing in America today.

Another lesson that my father impressed upon me is "Waste not and want not!" I remember we were not allowed to simply throw orange peels into the fire on a winter's night because the livestock,[1] particularly cows, would relish the peels. Life was really hard growing up on the farm in the 1920s through the 1940s. We worked from sun up to sun down with little money or time for play.

---

[1] *Livestock* means farm animals.

▼ Comprehension Questions

Discuss this story in pairs or small groups.

1. Where did Becky grow up?

2. How many siblings did Becky have?

3. What did Becky do growing up?

4. What lessons did Becky's father teach her?

5. What was the most interesting point for you in this reading?

▼ Reading Comprehension: True or False?

Read the sentences, and decide whether they are true or false based on the information in the story. Write T for true or F for false.

_____ 1. Becky grew up in North Alabama.

_____ 2. Becky worked on a farm when she was growing up.

_____ 3. Becky's family was rich.

_____ 4. The cows would eat orange peels.

_____ 5. Becky's father believed it was important to always do a job very well.

Cultural Application

A focus on efficiency and practicality means that Americans place less emphasis on emotional decisions. You will find that Americans may make decisions based on what is more practical. They will also want to make the best use of time. This means that when you ask Americans how they're doing, their response might imply that they are quite busy with lots going on in their life. Being busy is a "good thing" in U.S. American culture. Americans are considered to be some of the hardest working people, with much focus placed on work. This means you may be expected to put in long hours at work too and to accomplish quite a bit in the time you are working, meaning that you have something to show for your time and work.

▶ Vocabulary Exercise

These words appeared in the reading. This activity helps you see how well you understood the vocabulary words. Circle the answer that most closely matches the meaning of the word. If there are any you don't know, add them to your vocabulary notebook.

1. impressed upon

My father impressed upon me this lesson. . . .

impressed upon means

a. mark

b. fix firmly in mind

c. move

d. remember

2. waste

"Waste not and want not!"

waste means

a. use carelessly

b. use wisely

c. not use

d. throw away

3. chores

We all had to work in the fields and share chores of every day living.

chores means

a. products

b. pieces

c. jobs

d. routine tasks

▶ Vocabulary Usage

Now, it's your turn to practice using these vocabulary words. Choose at least two vocabulary words, and write your own sentences using these new words in your vocabulary notebook.

▼ Writing/Speaking Practice

Choose one or more of these topics to write about or discuss in pairs or small groups.

1. Explain a proverb that is important to you.

2. What are some lessons you learned about life when you were growing up? What were you taught by family members and elders?

3. What is your opinion about thriftiness—how important is it to save? How important is it to Americans now to be thrifty and save?

4. What did you learn growing up about being thrifty? Do you like to save things, recycle them, or throw them away?

▼ Real Life Application: Interacting with U.S. Americans

Activity 1

Ask a few U.S. Americans these questions, and then report back to your class.

1. What are two or three proverbs that are really important to you?

2. What are some lessons about life that you learned from your family?

3. How thrifty do you think Americans are? Do you personally like to save things, recycle, or throw things away?

Activity 2

Visit a thrift store or go to a yard sale. Make a list of some of the items you find at these places. What do these items say about their owners? Share that list in class.

Part 2

▼ Pre-Reading Activities

Discuss these questions in pairs or small groups.

1. Find Mississippi on a map. What do you know about Mississippi?

2. What kind of sports do you like?

3. What sports are important in the U.S.?

4. Have you ever played on a sports team? If so, what was your experience?

▼ Vocabulary Prediction

Predict the meaning of these vocabulary words found in the story before you read the story. The word is provided in a sentence or phrase from the story. After you have predicted the meaning, then look up the word in a dictionary, and write the definition.

1. **forced integration**—*In the late 1960s and early 1970s, forced integration of the public schools in Mississippi brought white and black children together. . . .*

   Prediction: Forced integration means _____

   Definition: _____

2. **bind**—*The people in small towns of Mississippi in many instances have little to bind them. . . .*

   Prediction: Bind means _____

   Definition: _____

3. **mascot**—*What matters is that they are all Lions or Eagles or Chiefs or whatever other mascot they represent.*

   Prediction: Mascot means _____

   Definition: _____

4. **renewed**—*Yes, each September, my faith in the hope of our future in Mississippi and the United States is renewed. . . .*

Prediction: **Renewed** means _____

Definition: _____

Cultural Note: Competition and Teamwork

There is a general belief in the U.S. that competition brings out the best, including working together on teams. Here is a story that illustrates both competition and teamwork.

Steve's Story—Jackson, Mississippi

Athletics and particularly high school football unites people of different colors, socio-economic[1] levels and other factors that make them different individually. In the late 1960s and early 1970s, forced integration of the public schools in Mississippi brought white and black children together in situations that were viewed as "tense" at least. Magically when those black and white young men donned their helmets and shoulder pads and uniforms and became united in an effort to seek victory on Friday nights, the only color that mattered was the color of your jersey.[2] White hands snapped the ball to black hands and black bodies cleared paths for white runners. White coaches yelled instructions at black players and black coaches yelled instructions at white players and black daddies cheered for white players just as the white daddies cheered for the black young me. The people in small towns of Mississippi in many instances have little to bind them as poverty and crime force them to move to places where there are more and better jobs. But on Friday nights in the fall in places such as Mize, Weir, Pontotoc, South Panola,

---

[1] *socio-economic* refers to different levels or classes of people based on their income (money).
[2] *jersey* means shirt, usually a team shirt.

Wiggins, Natchez, Bruce, and Pelahatchie there are only two divisions of people—our team and yours—the guys with the red jerseys and the guys with the white jerseys. That is all that matters—not whether Dontae's daddy has no job or Brian's daddy is the mayor or that Monty lives on the north side of the tracks and Scott lives in a big house on the hill. What matters is they are all Lions or Eagles or Chiefs or whatever other mascot they represent.

Yes, each September my faith in the hope of our future in Mississippi and the United States is renewed through the efforts of young men playing a game. All of us in America can learn from these young people in helmets, pads and jerseys. We can learn we are all people who have common goals and need to work together in all that we do.

▼ Comprehension Questions

Discuss this story in pairs or small groups.

1. What happens every September in Mississippi?

2. What happened in the early 1970s?

3. What brought white and black youth together in the 1970s?

4. What is important in football, according to Steve?

5. What gives Steve hope about the future?

6. What can we learn from football teams? From other sports?

7. What was the most interesting point for you in this reading?

▶ Reading Comprehension: True or False?

Read the sentences, and decide whether they are true or false based on the information in the story. Write T for true or F for false.

_____ 1. Football is played on Friday night.

_____ 2. Black fathers cheer for white players.

_____ 3. It matters what size house the players live in.

_____ 4. Football can teach the importance of working together.

Cultural Application

Given this focus on competition in U.S. American culture, it may seem that cooperation is de-emphasized in favor of competition. This means in work settings, members of a team will cooperate with each other, but they may also compete with other teams. This even may be displayed in personal relationships, with friends sometimes trying to outdo one another to see who can have the better job, the bigger house, and the nicer car. This means that neighbors may even try to compete more with each other than to help each other. Always try to do and be your best.

▛ Vocabulary Exercise

These words appeared in the reading. This activity helps you see how well you understood the vocabulary words. Circle the answer that most closely matches the meaning of the word. If there are any you don't know, add them to your vocabulary notebook.

1. athletics

Athletics and particularly high school football unites people of different colors. . . .

athletics means

a. active

b. inactive

c. table games

d. sports games

2. tense

. . . forced integration of the public schools in Mississippi brought white and black people together in situations that were viewed as "tense" at least.

tense means

a. relaxed

b. strained

c. calm

d. still

3. magically

Magically when those black and white young men donned their helmets and shoulder pads and uniforms and became united. . . .

magically means

a. sadly

b. miraculously

c. not normally

d. normally

4. poverty

The people in small towns of Mississippi in many instances have little to bind them as poverty and crime force them to move. . . .

poverty means

a. plenty

b. little

c. rich

d. poor

5. represent

What matters is they are all Lions or Eagles or Chiefs or whatever other mascot they represent.

represent means

a. show

b. have

c. made

d. symbolize

▛ Vocabulary Usage

Now, it's your turn to practice using these vocabulary words. Choose at least two vocabulary words, and write your own sentences using these new words in your vocabulary notebook.

▛ Writing/Speaking Practice

Choose one or more of these topics to write about or discuss in pairs or small groups.

1. What is your favorite sport? What do you like about it?

2. Describe an experience you have had with teamwork. Have you ever been on a team (sports or non-sports team)? What was that experience like for you?

3. What makes for a successful team? What do you think helps a team work well together?

4. What did you learn growing up about competition and cooperation? Which do you personally prefer, and why?

▸ Real Life Application: Interacting with U.S. Americans

Activity 1

Ask a few U.S. Americans these questions, and then report back to your class.

1. Have you ever been on a team (sports or non-sports)? If so, tell me about that experience.

2. What do you think makes a team work well together?

3. What is your opinion about competition and cooperation?

4. What advice would you give to someone about working on a team?

Activity 2

If possible, attend a team sporting event (for example, basketball, soccer, football, etc.) and write down what you observe about the sports teams. Who is on the team, what backgrounds do they have, do they all speak the same language, how well do they seem to work together, what could make them even more successful? You could also watch a team sport on TV. Write up a summary of your observation and bring it to class.

Activity 3

Look through magazines and newspapers for examples of competition or cooperation. You could also look on the Internet for such examples and print them. Cut out those examples and bring them to class to discuss.

▶ End-of-Unit Activities

List at least one new cultural insight you gained from this unit that helps you understand U.S. American culture a little better.

Based on the information in this unit, write at least one or two things that you will do or that you want to remember to improve your interactions with U.S. Americans.

Turn to the Notes section at the end of this textbook (page 206), and complete the section related to Unit 7.

UNIT **8**

A Look at the Midwest

Part 1

Pre-Reading Activities

Discuss these questions in pairs or small groups.

1. Find Indiana on the map. What do you know about Indiana?
2. How important is time to you?
3. What do you think Americans believe about time?

Vocabulary Prediction

Predict the meaning of these vocabulary words found in the story before you read the story. The word is provided in a sentence or phrase from the story. After you have predicted the meaning, then look up the word in a dictionary, and write the definition.

1. **chairman**—*I'm chairman, CEO*[1] *and founder of a trucking company with 3,500 employees. . . .*

   Prediction: Chairman means ______________________________

   Definition: ______________________________________

2. **pester**—*I am known around the company as the "Great Pesterer". . . .*

   Prediction: Pester means ______________________________

   Definition: ______________________________________

[1] *Chairperson* is the more appropriate term to use today.

3. unfair—*I felt like the world was unfair to me. . . .*

Prediction: Unfair means _____

Definition: _____

Cultural Note: Time

Mainstream U.S. culture is time-oriented. Time is considered to be valuable and limited. The story that follows is an example of how time is valued.

Stephen's Story—Indianapolis, Indiana

I'm Chairman, CEO[1] and founder of a trucking company with 3,500 employees, based in Indianapolis. I drive people crazy, because of my passion for time. I hate wasting time, I never lie on a couch looking at the ceiling. When I ask someone in our company to do something, what would normally take a couple of days to do, I expect to be done in a day. When someone says "I'll get back to you," I will probably ask that person how they're doing on the answer four or five times before they respond. I am known around the company as the "Great Pesterer," as time is so important to me.

I couldn't wait to get through school. I skipped eighth grade, and skipped my senior year at Cornell University, because I couldn't wait to get started in life.

I was born in Brooklyn, New York, in 1940. My father was a taxi driver, who died when I was 21 years old. In 1946, my mother died of cancer. I had just turned six years old. The only scene I remember of my mother was when she was put into an ambulance to go to the hospital. She never came home, as she died about two weeks later. In those days, little kids were not allowed in patient rooms. I never saw her again.

---

[1] CEO stands for Chief Executive Officer, which means the "boss" of the company.

I was the only kid in my class at grade school without a mother. Those were the days before divorces. I felt like the world was unfair to me, because I didn't have a mother. My father, as a taxi driver, only made money when he was driving the taxi, and to me seemed to work all the time.

Now at 66 years old, I realize that through her death, my mother gave me a gift. That gift was the understanding, at the age of six, that all God gave us in life is time. Use it. Be passionate about it. Don't lose it or waste it. That passion made me successful in life, and I thank my mother for that gift.

▼ Comprehension Questions

Discuss this story in pairs or small groups.

1. What does Stephen do?

2. Where was he born?

3. What did his father do?

4. What happened to his parents?

5. What gift did his mother give to Stephen?

6. What is so important to Stephen? What advice does he give?

7. What was the most interesting point for you in this reading?

Cultural Application

Generally, in U.S. American culture, it's important to be on time. This means if you are invited to an event or have an appointment, you should plan to at least be there by the time stated, although it depends on the situation. For example, if you've been invited to a home for dinner at 6 PM, it's important for you to arrive at 6:00 PM or just a couple minutes after that (do not come early!). If you have a doctor's appointment, it's best to arrive 10 to 15 minutes early. If it's a party, you should still arrive within a half-hour of the start time. For work, you need to be there a little before your work time starts, generally. Parties and social events often have ending times in the U.S., so it's important to be aware of when others are leaving and not stay too long. If you're going to be late, it's best to call to let people know you're delayed. Paying attention to time in the U.S. is often quite important.

▼ Vocabulary Exercise

These words appeared in the reading. This activity helps you see how well you understood the vocabulary words. Circle the answer that most closely matches the meaning of the word. If there are any you don't know, add them to your vocabulary notebook.

1. **passion**

   That passion made me successful in life. . . .

   passion means
   a. not caring
   b. little feeling
   c. strong feeling
   d. not feeling

2. **get back to (someone)**

   . . . "I'll get back to you". . . .

   get back to someone means
   a. respond later to that person
   b. respond now to that person
   c. don't respond
   d. go visit that person

3. **skip**

I skipped eighth grade. . . .

skip means

a. pass over

b. include

c. jump

d. hop

4. **scene**

The only scene I remember of my mother. . . .

scene means

a. situation

b. see

c. show

d. performance

5. **divorce**

Those were the days before divorces. . . .

divorce means

a. married

b. no longer married

c. dating

d. separated

▸ Vocabulary Usage

Now, it's your turn to practice using these vocabulary words. Choose at least two vocabulary words, and write your own sentences using these new words in your vocabulary notebook.

▼ Writing/Speaking Practice

Choose one or more of these topics to write about or discuss in pairs or small groups.

1. Discuss your opinion about time.

2. Compare time in another country to time in the U.S.—do people think about time in a similar way or different way? Explain your answer.

3. What is something you can't wait to do?

4. What does it take to be successful in life?

▼ Real Life Application: Interacting with U.S. Americans

Activity 1

Ask a few U.S. Americans these questions, and then report back to your class.

1. What are your thoughts about time and schedules? Do you have enough time?

2. How important is it to be on time?

3. What do you do in your free time?

4. What is important to be successful in life?

Activity 2

Look through magazines and newspapers (or online) for any articles that mention time. Collect examples of schedules—work schedules, sports schedules, entertainment schedules, and so on from newspapers, colleagues, neighbors, or online. Bring these items to class to share what you found. You could also write a brief essay about what these articles and schedules tell you about U.S. American culture.

Part 2

▼ Pre-Reading Activities

Discuss these questions in pairs or small groups.

1. What have you read or heard about the Midwest part of the United States? Talk about someone you know who is from that part of the U.S. Find Missouri on the United States map. What do you know about Missouri?

2. What was school like for you when you were growing up?

3. What do you think school was like in the United States in the first half of the twentieth century? What is school like now in the U.S.?

4. What are teachers like in another culture? In the U.S.?

▼ Vocabulary Prediction

Predict the meaning of these vocabulary words found in the story before reading the story. The word is provided in a sentence or phrase from the story. After you have predicted the meaning, then look up the word in a dictionary, and write the definition.

1. recess— . . . *but made school fun by playing games with us at recess.* . . .

   Prediction: Recess means _____

   Definition: _____

2. project—*She was not only a good educator but made school fun by playing games with us at recess, having neat art projects.* . . .

   Prediction: Project means _____

   Definition: _____

3. browse— . . . *We could browse through the books and check them out.* . . .

   Prediction: Browse means _____

   Definition: _____

Cultural Note: Informality

In the U.S., informality is often preferred. This means people may use first names instead of family names (as in the stories in this book). It also means that teachers may interact with students on a more informal basis than in some cultures. The story that follows is an example of a school room from a long time ago and how the teacher interacted with her students.

Shirley's Story—Kansas City, Missouri

I attended Oak Grove School which was a one-room school house a short distance from my grandparents' farm on a dirt road that often was drifted full of snow in the winter and we had to get to school either by horses or walking. We had one teacher who taught all eight grades. She was not only a good educator but made school fun by playing games with us at recess, having neat art projects, and encouraging us to read by having the "Book Mobile" come to our school often. The "Book Mobile" was a truck with shelves in the enclosed back that were lined with lots of books. We could browse through the books and check them out and we got reading achievement certificates from the state.

I have wonderful childhood memories of a loving, kind, Christian family and although everyone worked hard, it seems to me that life was good and perhaps less stressful. Neighbors and family took care of each other and the church provided not only a place of worship but also a place for social gatherings.

▸ Comprehension Questions

Discuss this story in pairs or small groups.

1. Describe Shirley's school.

2. How did Shirley get books to read?

3. What did Shirley get after reading books?

4. Where did Shirley and her family go for social gatherings?

5. What was the most interesting point for you in this reading?

▸ Reading Comprehension: True or False?

Read the sentences, and decide whether they are true or false based on the information in the story. Write T for true or F for false.

_____ 1. Shirley had several teachers.

_____ 2. Shirley's grandparents lived on a farm.

_____ 3. Shirley went to the local library to check out books.

_____ 4. Shirley and her family went to church for social gatherings.

_____ 5. Shirley liked her teacher because the teacher lectured all the time.

Cultural Application

Informality in the United States is a way to break down barriers between people and to try to show equality, which is highly valued in U.S. culture. Don't be surprised if you are frequently called by your first name. In fact, don't be surprised if your teacher prefers you to call him or her by first name; your teacher may find the use of a title such as Teacher a bit odd in U.S. culture. (U.S. Americans do not generally use a title such as Teacher when speaking directly with someone in that position.) Sometimes such informality can be viewed by those from other cultures as disrespectful, but in the U.S. informality is not usually meant to be disrespectful.

▛ Vocabulary Exercise

These words appeared in the reading. This activity helps you see how well you understood the vocabulary words. Circle the answer that most closely matches the meaning of the word. If there are any you don't know, add them to your vocabulary notebook.

1. **lined with**

   . . . shelves in the enclosed back that were lined with lots of books.

   lined with means
   a. be in order
   b. arranged
   c. filled
   d. unarranged

2. **achievement**

   . . . and we got reading achievement certificates from the state.

   achievement means
   a. failure
   b. accomplishment
   c. performance
   d. disappointment

3. **took care of**

   Neighbors and family took care of each other . . .

   took care of means
   a. thought about
   b. forgot
   c. supported
   d. remembered

4. **social gatherings**

   . . . the church provided not only a place of worship, but also a place for social gatherings.

   social gatherings means
   a. religious meetings
   b. work
   c. business meetings
   d. times with friends

5. **stressful**

   . . . it seems to me that life was good and perhaps less stressful.

   stressful means
   a. filled with mental tension and worry
   b. enjoyable
   c. filled with anger and unhappiness
   d. filled with activity

▸ Vocabulary Usage

Now, it's your turn to practice using these vocabulary words. Choose at least two vocabulary words, and write your own sentences using these new words in your vocabulary notebook.

▸ Writing/Speaking Practice

Choose one or more of these topics to write about or discuss in pairs or small groups.

1. What was it like to go to school when you were growing up?

2. Tell me about your favorite teacher—what was that teacher like? What did you like most about this teacher?

3. What are some differences and similarities between an American classroom and a classroom in your country? What are some ways that the teachers are similar or different? What are the attitudes toward teachers? What are some ways that the learning is similar or different?

◤ Real Life Application: Interacting with U.S. Americans

Activity 1

Ask a few U.S. Americans these questions, and then report back to your class. Think about the answers you receive. Do you notice any similarities in the answers? What does this say about how Americans view teachers?

1. What was it like to go to school when you were growing up?

2. Tell me about your favorite teacher—what was that teacher like? How did you address that teacher? What did you like most about this teacher?

3. How have attitudes toward school and teachers changed over the years? Do you find U.S. culture to be more formal or informal? Explain.

Activity 2

If you don't already have a library card to your local public library, be sure to get one. Then check out some books about life in the U.S. a long time ago. One series that is good to read is the *Little House on the Prairie* books by Laura Ingalls Wilder, which are based on a true story. These books will give you an idea of what teaching and learning used to be like in the United States a long time ago.

▼ End-of-Unit Activities

List at least one new cultural insight you gained from this unit that helps you understand U.S. American culture a little better.

Based on the information in this unit, write at least one or two things that you will do or that you want to remember to improve your interactions with U.S. Americans.

Turn to the Notes section at the end of this textbook (page 206), and complete the section related to Unit 8.

A Look at the Great Lakes

Part 1

▼ Pre-Reading Activities

Discuss these questions in pairs or small groups.

1. Find Michigan on a map. What do you know about Michigan? About the Great Lakes area?

2. How do you define family? How many people are in your family?

3. How do you think U.S. Americans define family?

▼ Vocabulary Prediction

Predict the meaning of these vocabulary words found in the story before you read the story. The word is provided in a sentence or phrase from the story. After you have predicted the meaning, then look up the word in a dictionary, and write the definition.

1. **support**—*We trust one another and show support.*

   Prediction: Support means _____

   Definition: _____

2. **spiritual**—*Our family is very spiritual. We attend a small non-denominational church in my hometown.*

   Prediction: Spiritual means _____

   Definition: _____

3. habits— . . . *I got myself out of the bad habits I was in.*

   Prediction: Habits mean _____

   Definition: _____

4. turning point—*Family was always important to me, but this was the turning point in my heart.*

   Prediction: Turning point means _____

   Definition: _____

Cultural Note: Family

For U.S. Americans, family usually means the immediate family, namely parents, children, and grandparents. Often, family members do not live all in one place—family members sometimes live in different states. The next story gives an example of how one American thinks about family.

Hannah's Story—Gwinn, Michigan

Ever since I was little, family has been a big part of my life. The holidays are spent at my grandparents' house on both my dad and mom's side of the family. I have tons of cousins so there was never a dull moment. The laughter and fun that came with the shared times made our family grow strong. We trust one another and show support. Without the love of my family, who knows where I would be today.

Our family is very spiritual. We attend a small non-denominational[1] church in my hometown. At one point my dad's whole side of the family went to the same church together. My grandma and grandpa live their lives through Christ each and everyday. Their influence, along with my parents, changed my whole life. I started to attend church again and I got myself out of the bad habits I was in. Family was always important to me, but this was the turning point in my heart.

---

[1] *non-denominational* refers to a Christian church that does not belong to a denomination such as Baptist, Lutheran, Methodist, and so on.

I began to see the small things in our family that made it so special. I realized that not everyone has a family at all, let alone a big and loving one. There's nothing more that pleases me than to be with my family. I soak in every word they say and every smile that shines. I believe that the power of family is so important in who I am. They will always be there to support me and to make me feel safe. I am loved and important, secure and complete. This is what I believe and nothing will ever change it.

▶ Comprehension Questions

Discuss this story in pairs or small groups.

1. Where does Hannah celebrate the holidays?

2. How many cousins does Hannah have?

3. What do you know about Hannah's grandparents?

4. What changed Hannah's life?

5. What makes Hannah happy?

6. What was the most interesting point for you in this reading?

Cultural Application

In the United States, you will find many different examples of "family." Some are "blended" families, meaning families who've come together because of different divorces and re-marriages, while others are "single parent" families in which only one parent is there. Still others may be "same sex" families where there are partners of the same sex living together, and some may be "traditional families" of father, mother, and children together. On more rare occasions, you may find "extended families" living together—these families may include grandparents, aunts/uncles, cousins, and so on. Just keep an open mind about definitions of "family" in the United States, and don't expect families to conform to one certain way.

▟ Vocabulary Exercise

These words appeared in the reading. This activity helps you see how well you understood the vocabulary words. Match the vocabulary word with the word that most closely matches the meaning. If there are any you don't know, add them to your vocabulary notebook.

_____ 1. dull   a. safe

_____ 2. influence   b. absorb

_____ 3. realized   c. boring

_____ 4. soak in   d. to have an effect on

_____ 5. secure   e. to understand

▟ Vocabulary Usage

Now, it's your turn to practice using these vocabulary words. Choose at least two vocabulary words, and write your own sentences using these new words in your vocabulary notebook.

▟ Writing/Speaking Practice

Choose one or more of these topics to write about or discuss in pairs or small groups.

1. Based on your experiences, what should others know about families? How would you describe families?

2. Compare families in the U.S. to families in another culture with which you are familiar.

3. Choose a holiday you celebrate with family and explain how you celebrate it.

Real Life Application: Interacting with U.S. Americans

Activity 1

Ask a few U.S. Americans these questions, and then report back to your class. Compare answers with other classmates. Then, talk or write about what the differences are between families in the U.S. and in other cultures. For example, when U.S. Americans talk about their families, do they tell you about cousins, aunts, and uncles, or do they mostly talk about children, parents, brothers, and sisters?

1. Tell me about different kinds of families in the U.S.
2. Tell me briefly about your family.
3. Tell me about a holiday you celebrate with your family.

Activity 2

Look through magazines and cut out pictures of families to bring to class to share. Watch TV shows and write down the kinds of families that are shown in those programs—what family members are part of those families (for example, parents, grandparents, aunts and uncles)? How are the families in these magazine pictures and TV shows similar or different from American families you know? From families in other cultures?

Part 2

Pre-Reading Activities

Discuss these questions in pairs or small groups.

1. What do you know about high school students in the U.S.?
2. If you've ever been in a difficult situation, were you able to get out of it or change it? If so, how?
3. In other cultures, when can children move out of the house and live on their own?

Vocabulary Prediction

Predict the meaning of these vocabulary words found in the story before you read the story. The word is provided in a sentence or phrase from the story. After you have predicted the meaning, then look up the word in a dictionary and write the definition.

1. **verge**—*My parents fought constantly and were on the verge of a divorce.*

   Prediction: Verge means ____________________________

   Definition: ____________________________________

2. **bonding**— . . . *every day brings new prospects for bonding. . . .*

   Prediction: Bonding means __________________________

   Definition: ____________________________________

3. **quality**— . . . *not allowing my environment to affect that quality of my life. . . .*

   Prediction: Quality means ___________________________

   Definition: ____________________________________

Cultural Note: Personal Control, Independence

In the U.S., there is a general belief that people can or should control their own environment and their own futures. This is connected to independence, with the success of the individual being most important. The next story is an example of one U.S. American who took control of her environment and made a better future for herself.

Amber's Story—Middleville, Michigan

I believe that whatever environment you are raised in doesn't have to affect the quality of your life. When I was sixteen, my home-life was not stable to say the least. My parents fought constantly and were on the verge of a divorce. Most of the time, with me being the oldest, the anger they were feeling for each other was taken out in verbal means with me. I was constantly working in the household trying to pick up the slack[1] and keep everyone happy so that maybe the problems would just go away. I was an all (A)[2] student in my junior[3] year in high school with perfect attendance.[4] I held a part-time job and played sometimes two sports a semester.

I decided that my parents' problems were not going to interfere with the quality of my life. Luckily, I had my grandma and my uncle who lived only a couple of miles away so I decided, when I got enough courage, that I was going to ask if I could stay with them until I graduated and moved away to college. With them being so close it allowed me to transition my schedule easily with sports, work, and school. Finally, after a month of soul searching[5] and courage building, I moved in with my relatives. Now that my stress had diminished,[6] I continued my focus on my studies, work and sports in my new nurturing and caring environment. My high school career brought many opportunities with my grades and my community involvement and allowed me to attend college the year after I graduated.

With this experience of taking a stand[7] and not allowing my environment to affect that quality of my life I actually am more self-sufficient. At

---

[1] *pick up the slack* is an idiomatic expression that means to do the work that others don't do.
[2] *all A* refers to the top grade a student can achieve in a U.S. classroom. *All A* means the student gets outstanding marks in every class.
[3] *junior year* is the next to last year in high school.
[4] *perfect attendance* in this case means not missing any days of school during the school year; awards are often given for perfect attendance.
[5] *soul searching* refers to a time of deep thinking about a situation or issue in order to come to some resolution.
[6] *diminished* means reduced or lessened.
[7] *taking a stand* is an idiomatic expression that means to take firm action on an issue or situation.

the age of twenty-two, I own my own home with my husband of three years and we are expecting our first child. I have a wonderful career with a major insurance[8] company and I have my life ahead of me. My family ties with my parents are still demanding but every day brings new prospects[9] for bonding. I did not allow myself to be a victim of circumstance.[10] I made my future what I wanted it to be. I believe, like the old saying, *If there is a will there is a way*, and I had the will. I am now on my way!

▼ Comprehension Questions

Discuss this story in pairs or small groups.

1. What do you know about Amber's home life?

2. What did Amber do in high school?

3. What problem did Amber encounter?

4. What did she decide to do about this problem?

5. What does Amber do now?

6. What was the most interesting point for you in this reading?

Cultural Application

There is a general belief in U.S. American culture that individuals can and should take control over their own futures, that they shouldn't let life circumstances control what happens to them. That means U.S. Americans may like stories about individuals who changed their life from one of poverty to success, about immigrants who came to the U.S. and made a better life for themselves. This also means that you may find Americans to be energetic and goal-oriented. And you may be asked about what your own goals are and what you hope to achieve, so be ready with an answer. This also means that Americans will expect you to take control of your life and make it what you want by archieving your goals.

---

[8] *insurance company* is a company that sells insurance policies that will help pay for difficult situations such as car accidents, surgery in hospitals, etc.
[9] *prospects* mean possibilities.
[10] *victim of circumstance* means to be hurt by the situation.

▶ Vocabulary Exercise

These words appeared in the reading. This activity helps you see how well you understood the vocabulary words. Match the vocabulary word with the word that most closely matches the meaning. If there are any you don't know, add them to your vocabulary notebook.

_____ 1. environment   a. always

_____ 2. constantly   b. change

_____ 3. interfere   c. bravery

_____ 4. courage   d. be an obstacle/prevent

_____ 5. transition   e. surroundings

_____ 6. self-sufficient   f. independent

▶ Vocabulary Usage

Now, it's your turn to practice using these vocabulary words. Choose at least two vocabulary words, and write your own sentences using these new words in your vocabulary notebook.

▶ Writing/Speaking Practice

Choose one or more of these topics to write about or discuss in pairs or small groups.

1. Discuss Amber's situation and how it would be resolved in other cultures. For example, would a child be allowed to move in with other relatives?

2. Discuss the differences and similarities between independence in the U.S. and independence in another culture.

3. What is your opinion about being independent? Do you think it is possible to change your situation in life? Please explain.

◤ Real Life Application: Interacting with U.S. Americans

Activity 1

Ask a few U.S. Americans these questions, and then report back to your class

1. How important is it to be independent in the U.S.?

2. Do you think it's possible to change one's situation in life? Please explain.

3. How was the idea of independence communicated to you when you were growing up? Can you give some examples of what you were allowed to do or encouraged to do by yourself when you were growing up?

4. Can you think of any proverbs or sayings that relate to being self-sufficient and independent, or having control over one's environment?

Activity 2

Find three to five examples of U.S. Americans who have changed their lives for the better despite their situation. These can be local people or famous people. You can research this through the library, the Internet, or by talking with others. Bring your list to class with the Americans' names and a brief summary of how they each made their life better. Discuss how these examples are similar or different from examples in your own culture.

▟ End-of-Unit Activities

List at least one new cultural insight you gained from this unit that helps you understand U.S. American culture a little better.

Based on the information in this unit, write at least one or two things that you will do or that you want to remember to improve your interactions with U.S. Americans.

Turn to the Notes section at the end of this textbook (page 207), and complete the section related to Unit 9.

A Look at the Great Plains

Part 1

▼ Pre-Reading Activities

Discuss these questions in pairs or small groups.

1. Find Oklahoma on a map. What do you know about Oklahoma?

2. Talk about your family background. Where were your parents born and raised?

3. What did you do for fun when you were growing up?

4. What chores (routine tasks) did you do when you were growing up?

▼ Vocabulary Prediction

Predict the meaning of these vocabulary words found in the story before you read the story. The word is provided in a sentence or phrase from the story. After you have predicted the meaning, then look up the word in a dictionary, and write the definition.

1. **devout**—*My parents were devout Christians.* . . .

   Prediction: Devout means _____

   Definition: _____

2. **harvest**—*Summer was a very busy with harvest time.* . . .

   Prediction: Harvest means _____

   Definition: _____

3. pasture— . . . *papa would play softball in the pasture with us.*

Prediction: Pasture means _____

Definition: _____

Cultural Note: Volunteerism, Action-Oriented

In the U.S., it is quite common to find Americans volunteering their time in the community, particularly given the value placed on being action-oriented. This interest in volunteering sometimes comes from religious beliefs or from a desire to help make the world a better place by helping others. This story is an example of one American's religious faith and her volunteer experience.

Edith's Story—Cloud Chief, Oklahoma

I was born into a family of German background. My father knew German from his birth, and learned English in public school. My mother only knew English which is what I learned. My parents were devout Christians, living on their own farm. All of us learned farming but most of all we learned Christianity. We had nothing modern in our home. We each knew our regular chores: milking cows, separating milk and cream, feeding calves, chickens, pigs and horses. When the morning chores were done, we would gather around the breakfast table for a time to worship before breakfast. During my growing up years there was only one morning in which morning worship was omitted—it was in harvest time. Summer was a very busy time with harvest time, raising a big garden and canning[1] vegetables for winter, canning fruit from the fruit trees on the farm. In winter time it was butchering[2] time in order to have our own beef and pork for meals.

---

[1] *canning* is a way of preserving the food in sealed glass jars.
[2] *butchering* means killing a pig or cow for food.

Our recreation was mostly playing outdoors games in summer. Sometimes we had a family picnic by the creek on our farm. Sometimes on Sunday afternoon, papa would play softball in the pasture with us. In winter, mama would sometimes play table games with us and help us make valentines (we never bought valentines). Sundays were very important days for almost the total community. This was a day of worship and rest. My parents tried to follow the teachings of our church . . . and the teaching of the New Testament. Many of our neighbors were aunts, uncles, and cousins. Most of the others were members of our church.

Later, I spent three years living and working in Europe. My work was volunteer and was done in three different countries—Germany, Austria, and Greece. I must say that for me I found so many more common things for each country than differences.

▼ Comprehension Questions

Discuss this story in pairs or small groups.

1. Where did Edith live?

2. What chores did she do?

3. What work was done in the summer and the winter?

4. What did Edith and her family do for fun?

5. Talk about the role that religion played in Edith's life when she was growing up.

6. What was the most interesting point for you in this reading?

▼ Reading Comprehension: True or False?

Read the sentences, and decide whether they are true or false based on the information in the story. Write T for true or F for false.

_____ 1. Edith's father spoke German.

_____ 2. Edith's family bought their meat from the market.

_____ 3. Edith was related to many of her neighbors.

_____ 4. Edith got paid for the work she did in Europe.

_____ 5. Edith's family was Jewish.

Cultural Application

Volunteering is often viewed by U.S. Americans as a way to take action and to help make the world a better place. In some cases, such volunteering is motivated by religious or personal beliefs. You may find U.S. Americans in your community who are actively volunteering with a variety of community organizations. Think about something you would like to take action on—something you would like to change. Regardless of whether volunteering is common to your own experience, you may want to consider ways in which you can volunteer in the local community where you are, if you have time and an interest in doing so. Volunteering can be a good way to practice language, meet others in the community, and help out the community in some way by taking action.

▶ Vocabulary Exercise

These words appeared in the reading. This activity helps you see how well you understood the vocabulary words. Circle the answer that most closely matches the meaning of the word. If there are any you don't know, add them to your vocabulary notebook.

1. background

I was born into a family of German background.

background means

a. scenery

b. total of one's experience

c. total of one's relatives

d. home

2. worship

. . . we would gather around the breakfast table for a time to worship before breakfast.

worship means

a. act of reverence for a divine being

b. act of irreverence for a divine being

c. act of respect

d. act of disrespect

3. omitted

. . . there was only one morning in which morning worship was omitted. . . .

omitted means

a. don't do

b. left out

c. included

d. inserted

4. recreation

Our recreation was mostly playing outdoor games in summer.

recreation means

a. rest

b. entertainment

c. work

d. leisure activity

5. volunteer

My work was volunteer. . . .

volunteer means

a. work with no pay

b. receive

c. give

d. work for pay

▛ Vocabulary Usage

Now, it's your turn to practice using these vocabulary words. Choose at least two vocabulary words, and write your own sentences using these new words in your vocabulary notebook.

▛ Writing/Speaking Practice

Choose one or more of these topics to write about or discuss in pairs or small groups.

1. Describe your family background. Where were your parents and grand-parents from?

2. What do you like to do for fun—now and when you were a child?

3. How important is religion in your life? What beliefs are important to you?

4. Have you ever volunteered anywhere? If so, please discuss what the experience was like for you.

5. Compare and contrast volunteering in the U.S. and in another culture.

▼ Real Life Application: Interacting with U.S. Americans

Activity 1

Ask a few U.S. Americans these questions, and then report back to your class. You may want to write a story about that person (similar to Edith's story). Bring the story to class to share.

1. Tell me about your family background, including any religious beliefs that have been important to your family.

2. What do you like to do for fun?

3. Have you ever volunteered anywhere? If so, please discuss what that experience was like for you and why you volunteered.

Activity 2

Find a place in the community where you can volunteer. This could be a place where you volunteer once a week or even once a month. Examples of some places to volunteer include at a nursing or retirement home, at a soup kitchen or homeless shelter, at a school, or with an organization like the American Red Cross. You can talk with your teacher about some places to volunteer or look in a newspaper or phone book. Volunteering in the United States is a wonderful way to meet U.S. Americans and to practice your English.

Part 2

▼ Pre-Reading Activities

Discuss these questions in pairs or small groups.

1. Find Nebraska on a map. What do you know about Nebraska?

2. What does it mean to be poor? Talk about what you know about poor people in the U.S.

3. What does it take to help make someone's life better?

◤ Vocabulary Prediction

Predict the meaning of these vocabulary words found in the story before you read the story. The word is provided in a sentence or phrase from the story. After you have predicted the meaning, then look up the word in a dictionary, and write the definition.

1. **predicament**— . . . *"poverty lag," a term my mother adapted to define our predicament.*

   Prediction: Predicament means _____

   Definition: _____

2. **instill**—*That mantra was instilled in us and guided my belief system.*

   Prediction: Instill means _____

   Definition: _____

3. **odd jobs**— . . . *my father, who had many children, had to do odd jobs and second jobs. . . .*

   Prediction: Odd jobs mean _____

   Definition: _____

4. **conscience**—*Those words burned into my conscience for years. . . .*

   Prediction: Conscience means _____

   Definition: _____

5. **humility**—*The humility of the meek illustrated true hospitality.*

   Prediction: Humility means _____

   Definition: _____

Cultural Note: Equality, Action-Oriented

In the U.S., there is a general belief that all people should have equal opportunities. When some persons don't have equal opportunities, Americans may take action to help others or to help themselves. In the story that follows, a man born into a poor family decides to help others—in other countries and in the U.S.

A-Jamal's Story—Omaha, Nebraska

As an African-American person I grew up in Omaha, Nebraska and experienced days where having enough food was a challenge for our family. My mother told us that there were factors beyond our control that contributed to our poverty. Social injustices and limited opportunities for social advancement[1] were "poverty lag," a term my mother adapted to define our predicament. She told us society was not fair to the poor and in spite of limited opportunities we had to be foot soldiers[2] for the poor. That mantra[3] was instilled in us and guided my belief system.

As a 12-year old adolescent I recalled going with my father to haul trash for extra money. He had just completed a hauling job for a white man when the man made a rude comment to my father. Those words burned into my conscience for years because of the tone and anger of that man.

For years I was ashamed of my father for putting himself in a predicament where a stranger would say harsh words to him—moreover in front of his son. After I had a family, I came to understand that my father, who had many children, had to do odd jobs and second jobs (with limited formal education) to put food on the table. Words can burn and sometimes it will be years before they are forgiven.

After graduation from the University of Nebraska, I joined the Peace Corps[4] and served two years in Botswana working with destitute[5] families in rural[6] areas living in the Kalahari Desert. It was in my travels that I found poor people demonstrating hospitality by sharing their evening meal of

---

[1] *social advancement* means to improve one's place in society.
[2] *foot soldiers* here refers to those who do necessary work (and in this story, it does not mean someone who carries a gun and fights in a military).
[3] *mantra* means a commonly repeated phrase.
[4] *Peace Corps* is a program of the United States government that sends volunteers to other countries, usually for two years, to help people there. For more information, see www.peacecorps.gov.
[5] *destitute* means poor.
[6] *rural* means in the country (not the city).

"Bogabe" (similar to oatmeal) with me. The humility of the meek[7] illustrated true hospitality. After my return to the United States and for the past twenty-three years, I have worked with the poor or less fortunate in a faith-based organization whose beliefs and mission[8] is to help transform society and improve lives.

◤ Comprehension Questions

Discuss this story in pairs or small groups.

1. What did A-Jamal experience growing up?

2. What did A-Jamal's mother mean by "poverty lag"?

3. What happened to A-Jamal's father, and how did A-Jamal feel about that?

4. What did A-Jamal do when he grew up?

5. How did the family in Botswana show hospitality to A-Jamal?

6. What was the most interesting point for you in this reading?

Cultural Application

In the U.S., circumstances are not often accepted as an "excuse" for why somebody can't do what he or she wants to do. The proverb of "where there's a will, there's a way" is strongly upheld in U.S. culture. In the U.S., there is a belief that one's circumstances in life can be changed and that one does not have to accept one's place in life. For example, if a person is born to a family without much money, he or she can change that—either by working hard, getting more knowledge or skills, or several other ways. For you, this means that you may encounter those who believe that you can be or achieve whatever you want to in American society. Think through specific steps on how you can improve your situation and help make your dreams come true.

---

[7] *meek* means gentle—here it describes poor people in Botswana.
[8] *mission* refers to purpose or work (of the organization).

◤ Vocabulary Exercise

These words appeared in the reading. This activity helps you see how well you understood the vocabulary words. Match the vocabulary word with the word that most closely matches the meaning. If there are any you don't know, add them to your vocabulary notebook.

_____ 1. challenge	a. embarrassed
_____ 2. contribute	b. change
_____ 3. injustice	c. add
_____ 4. adolescent	d. young person
_____ 5. ashamed	e. violation of what is right
_____ 6. transform	f. test
_____ 7. haul	g. carry

◤ Vocabulary Usage

Now, it's your turn to practice using these vocabulary words. Choose at least two vocabulary words, and write your own sentences using these new words in your vocabulary notebook.

◤ Writing/Speaking Practice

Choose one or more of these topics to write about or discuss in pairs or small groups.

1. How is hospitality shown in other cultures?

2. What do you think are some differences between hospitality in other cultures and in the U.S.?

3. Describe an unpleasant predicament you have seen or experienced.

4. What are your thoughts about poverty—in the U.S. and in another country?

5. What are some ways to help those who are less fortunate?

▶ Real Life Application: Interacting with U.S. Americans

Activity 1

Ask a few U.S. Americans these questions, and then report back to your class.

1. How do Americans show hospitality?

2. What is your opinion of racial relations in the U.S.? What do you know about racial relations?

3. What do you know specifically about poverty in the U.S.? In other countries?

4. What advice can you give about how to help those who are less fortunate?

Activity 2

Find out more about racial relations in the U.S. and social injustices that occur. Look through newspapers (or online) to find articles related to this topic. Watch a movie like "Mississippi Burning" to understand more about the history of racial relations. Go to the library, and ask the librarian to recommend some books on this topic.

Activity 3

Find out more about poverty in the U.S. What is the "poverty line"? What is the median income in your area? What services and agencies are available to help poor people? Research the answers to these questions at your local library or online. Write down what you learn and bring the information to class to share with your classmates.

▼ End-of-Unit Activities

List at least one new cultural insight you gained from this unit that helps you understand U.S. American culture a little better.

Based on the information in this unit, write at least one or two things you will do or that you want to remember to improve your interactions with U.S. Americans.

Turn to the Notes section at the end of this textbook (page 207), and complete the section related to Unit 10.

A Look at
the Southwest

Part 1

▼ Pre-Reading Activities

Discuss these questions in pairs or small groups.

1. Find New Mexico and Arizona on the United States map. Locate the Navajo Indian Reservation. Find more information about the Navajo tribe.[1]

2. Have you been to the American Southwest, or do you know someone who has been there?

3. What have you heard or read about Native Americans?

4. What do you know about traditions in Native American culture?

5. What traditions are important in your family?

6. What groups are you a member of?

---

[1] The Navajo tribe is the largest tribe of Native Americans living in the United States. There are many other native tribes that live in the U.S., including Cherokee, Apache, and Lakota.

▼ Vocabulary Prediction

Predict the meaning of these vocabulary words found in the story before you read the story. The word is provided in a sentence or phrase from the story. After you have predicted the meaning, then look up the definition in a dictionary, and write the definition.

1. **reservation**—*I grew up on the reservation . . .*

    Prediction: Reservation means _____

    Definition: _____

2. **ceremonial**—*We had to help a lot of our neighbors with the ceremonial activities.*

    Prediction: Ceremonial means _____

    Definition: _____

3. **orthopedics unit**—*Now I work as a nurse on an orthopedics unit.*

    Prediction: Orthopedics means _____

    Definition: _____

Cultural Note: Individuals and Groups

While the mainstream U.S. culture values individualism and each person being responsible for him- or herself, other cultures within the U.S. may adhere to a more group-oriented way of thinking, as shown in this Native American perspective on being a member of a tribe.

Marlene's Story—Lybrook, New Mexico

My name is Marlene. I live in the northwest corner of New Mexico. I am a member of the Navajo Tribe. The Navajo Reservation is near my home and surrounds the area where I live. I grew up on the reservation with my family who practiced traditional medicine. My family beliefs in the medicine men[1] were strong. We had to help a lot of our neighbors with the ceremonial activities. My uncle and grandmother were both practitioners of traditional medicine.[2] My mother used to have different healing ceremonies done for her. She would have me do most of the chores. I was responsible for raising my younger siblings.

I remember attending the church school. I did not speak a word of English. The things I remember from the school were a big green piano, Kool-Aid,[3] and cookies. Now I work as a nurse on an orthopedics unit.

▼ Comprehension Questions

Discuss this story in pairs or small groups.

1. Where does Marlene live?

2. What does Marlene do now?

3. What tradition was important to her family when she was growing up?

4. What are her memories of school?

5. What was the most interesting point for you in this reading?

---

[1] *medicine men* are often found in Native American tribes and are thought to be special healers—similar to medical doctors in the larger society.
[2] *traditional medicine* involves the use of ceremonies, rituals, and the use of natural plants in the healing process.
[3] *Kool-Aid* is a type of powdered drink that is added to water—it is popular with children and comes in different fruit flavors.

◤ Reading Comprehension: True or False?

Read the sentences, and decide whether they are true or false based on the information in the story. Write T for true or F for false.

_____ 1. Marlene spoke English well as a child.

_____ 2. Marlene is a Navajo Indian.

_____ 3. Marlene has older brothers and sisters.

_____ 4. Marlene's mother believes in traditional medicine.

_____ 5. Marlene is a nurse on an orthopedics unit.

Cultural Application: Individualism vs. Group Orientation

Often times in U.S. American culture, the focus is placed on the individual, in which there's a belief that if each person takes of him- or herself, everything will be OK. However, within this pattern of individualism found in U.S. culture, there are influences from other groups, such as Native Americans, where the focus is on the group. It is important to understand that while many Americans have been raised with a focus on the individual, there are some within the U.S. that see themselves as part of a group, and that fact is an important part of their identity.

▼ Vocabulary Exercise

These words appeared in the reading. This activity helps you see how well you understood the vocabulary words. Circle the answer that most closely matches the meaning of the word. If there are any you don't know, add them to your vocabulary notebook.

1. **surrounds**

   The Navajo Reservation is near my home and surrounds the area. . . .

   surrounds means

   a. encircles

   b. separates

   c. attacks

   d. protects

2. **healing**

   My mother used to have different healing ceremonies done for her.

   healing means

   a. to make sick

   b. to make well

   c. to celebrate

   d. to make peace

3. **practitioners**

   My uncle and grandmother were both practitioners. . . .

   practitioners means

   a. authorized medical doctors

   b. persons with acquired skills

   c. common persons with no skills

   d. everyday workers

4. **siblings**

   I was responsible for raising my younger siblings.

   siblings means

   a. cousins

   b. neighbors

   c. aunts and uncles

   d. sisters and brothers

▶ Vocabulary Usage

Now, it's your turn to practice using these vocabulary words. Choose at least two vocabulary words, and write your own sentences using these new words in your vocabulary notebook.

▶ Writing/Speaking Practice

Choose one or more of these topics to write about or discuss in pairs or small groups.

1. Is your identity associated with you as an individual or as being part of a group? Explain.

2. Describe a special tradition or ceremony in another culture.

3. What are your impressions of traditions in the United States? Have you ever seen a tradition or ceremony in the U.S.? If so, describe it. What U.S. American traditions or ceremonies would you like to learn more about?

▶ Real Life Application: Interacting with U.S. Americans

Activity 1

Ask a few U.S. Americans these questions, and then report back to your class.

1. How important is it to you to be part of a group in the U.S.? Is belonging to a group necessary to be successful here?

2. Which groups are you a member of?

3. Please tell me about one of the traditions or ceremonies that is important to your family, either now or when you were growing up.

4. What advice can you give to someone who wants to learn more about the traditions that are important to U.S. Americans?

Activity 2

Research information about Native American tribes. You can find out more about their history and traditions and the current situation. Bring this information to class and share it with your classmates; this can be done through a poster, a presentation, or by having your classmates participate in a traditional Native American game or activity.

Activity 3

Research information about a U.S. American tradition or ceremony that you would like to learn more about. This can include asking U.S. Americans about the tradition or ceremony, and even participating, if this is possible. Bring this information to class and share it with your classmates; this can be done through a poster, a presentation, or by having your classmates actually participate in an activity from the tradition or ceremony.

Part 2

▶ Pre-Reading Activities

Discuss these questions in pairs or small groups.

1. How many languages do you speak?

2. How important is language to one's identity?

3. Do you think it is important to speak one's own languages? Please explain.

▶ Vocabulary Prediction

Predict the meaning of these vocabulary words found in the story before reading the story. The word is provided in a sentence or phrase from the story. After you have predicted the meaning, then look up the word in a dictionary and write the definition.

1. **patients**—*I assisted the doctor and the nurse with the patients . . .*
   Prediction: Patients mean _____
   Definition: _____

2. **generations**—*The younger generations are losing . . .*
   Prediction: Generations means _____
   Definition: _____

3. **wisdom**—*They carry on the wisdom of the Navajo culture and traditions.*
   Prediction: Wisdom means _____
   Definition: _____

Cultural Note: Language

There are many languages spoken in the U.S., including Native American languages. Here is a story that shares the experience of maintaining one's own language.

Arlene's Story—Bloomfield, New Mexico

Ya'at'eeh (hello). My first introduction to the English language was when my parents enrolled me at the Lybrook Navajo Mission.[1] My native language was the Navajo language. My father, Juan, used to take my sister Frances and me on horseback to meet the bus every morning. I remember the hardest word to learn to pronounce was the word "blue." Because my mom was partially blind, my dad helped me fix my hair for school.

During the summer time, when my dad and grandparents found work in Colorado to do farm work, I remember interpreting for my grandmother in the conversations with the farmer. My first work experience was working at the Lybrook Mission as a medical aid. I assisted the doctor and the nurse with the patients and interpreted for the patients. Currently, I am working for . . . the Navajo Nation government. I am fluent in speaking the Navajo and English languages and am able to use the languages in my daily work and life. The younger generations are losing their Navajo language and their first language is the English language. We are trying to teach our children to speak the Navajo language, to promote the importance of preserving and learning the Navajo traditional culture and language. This is important in knowing their self-identity, the language, a way of life to make them a stronger person, which gives them a good foundation. They carry on the wisdom of the Navajo culture and traditions.

---

[1] A mission is similar to a school. It is usually organized by a religious group not originally from that area, and that group sends in volunteers to work with the Native Americans to teach them English, to provide medical aid, and to teach them about their religion—in this case, Christianity.

▶ Comprehension Questions

Discuss this story in pairs or small groups.

1. What languages does Arlene speak?

2. What is Arlene's main concern?

3. What did her dad and grandparents do in the summer? What did Arlene do then?

4. What does Arlene do now?

5. Why does Arlene think that speaking a native language is important?

6. What was the most interesting point for you in this reading?

Cultural Application

Even though English is spoken widely in the U.S. and in the world, there are still many different languages spoken in homes throughout the U.S. Think about the pros and cons of many different languages being spoken in the same society. And think about how learning a language and learning about culture are connected. In your workplace in the U.S., it's generally a good idea to refrain from speaking another language other than English unless you are expected to do so or unless your boss says it's OK.

▚ Vocabulary Exercise

These words appeared in the reading. This activity helps you see how well you understood the vocabulary words. Circle the answer that most closely matches the meaning of the word. If there are any you don't know, add them to your vocabulary notebook.

1. **partially**

   Because my mom was partially blind. . . .

   partially means
   a. mostly
   b. quite
   c. fully
   d. partly

2. **interpreting**

   I remember interpreting for my grandmother. . . .

   interpreting means
   a. singing
   b. translating
   c. listening
   d. playing

3. **promote**

   . . . to promote the importance of preserving and learning the Navajo traditional culture. . . .

   promote means
   a. find
   b. hide
   c. announce
   d. encourage

4. preserving

   . . . to promote the importance of preserving and learning. . . .

   preserving means
   a. discovering
   b. throwing away
   c. forgetting
   d. keeping

5. foundation

   . . . a way of life to make them a stronger person which gives them a good foundation.

   foundation means
   a. preparation
   b. base
   c. beginning
   d. part

▶ Vocabulary Usage

Now, it's your turn to practice using these vocabulary words. Choose at least two vocabulary words, and write your own sentences using these new words in your vocabulary notebook.

▶ Writing/Speaking Practice

Choose one or more of these topics to write about or discuss in pairs or small groups.

1. Write about the languages you speak. How did you learn them? How and where do you use the languages now?

2. Write about how you feel when you speak your language(s)—do you feel differently when you speak one or the other? How does the language change you? When and where do you speak your language(s)?

3. Write about your impressions of languages in the United States, including examples of immigrants you know who have been in the U.S. a long time. What languages do they speak?

4. Do you think it is important to learn different languages? Why or why not?

▼ Real Life Application: Interacting with U.S. Americans

Activity 1

Ask a few U.S. Americans these questions, and then report back to your class.

1. How many languages do you speak?

2. How important is it to preserve one's native language? What are some ways to do this?

3. How does speaking another language change who you are? Or does it?

4. What advice can you give to someone about learning another language and about maintaining one's own language?

Activity 2

Research the different languages spoken in the United States (or in your state)—both in the rural areas and in the cities. How many different languages are spoken where you live? Which ones are most prevalent (meaning, which ones occur most often)? What do you notice about immigrants in your area? How is this similar or different in another country?

◤ End-of-Unit Activities

List at least one new cultural insight you gained from this unit that helps you understand U.S. American culture a little better.

Based on the information in this unit, write one or two things that you will do or that you want to remember to improve your interactions with U.S. Americans.

Turn to the Notes section at the end of this textbook (page 208), and complete the section related to Unit 11.

A Look at the West

Part 1

▼ Pre-Reading Activities

Discuss these questions in pairs or small groups.

1. Find California on the map. What do you know about California?

2. What do you know about the way Japanese Americans were treated by the U.S. government during World War II?

3. What do you know about high school life in the U.S.?

4. What was secondary school like for you?

5. What do you think is meant by "civil rights"? What do you know about "civil rights"?

◤ Vocabulary Prediction

Predict the meaning of these vocabulary words found in the story before you read the story. The word is provided in a sentence or phrase from the story. After you have predicted the meaning, then look up the word in a dictionary and write out the definition.

1. **elder**—*During World War II, my elder family was imprisoned by their government.*

   Prediction: Elder means _____

   Definition: _____

2. **entitled**—*I was taught and I believed I was entitled to all of the rights guaranteed by the U.S. Constitution.*

   Prediction: Entitled means _____

   Definition: _____

3. **lawsuits**—*Now I am a Japanese American woman trial attorney representing plaintiffs in discrimination lawsuits against the government.*

   Prediction: Lawsuits mean _____

   Definition: _____

4. **imperfections**—*I still believe in my country with all its imperfections.*

   Prediction: Imperfections mean _____

   Definition: _____

Cultural Note: Patriotism

U.S. Americans are generally considered to be patriotic. Here is a story about one U.S. American who is loyal to the U.S., despite—or maybe because of—the experience of her family.

Patricia's Story—Davis, California

I was born in 1951, 6 years after my family was released from the Japanese American Internment Camps.[1] During World War II, my elder family was imprisoned by their government. After "camp," they felt ashamed, but still loyal to their country, America. My grandfather told me, "shi gata ganai"— it could not be helped. My grandmother, mother and father were born in America. I was born in America. My parents made me believe that I was the All American[2] girl.

I knew I looked different. I knew my last name was hard to pronounce because every new teacher struggled to say my name at roll call. I remember being a Brownie Girl Scout.[3] We wore our uniforms to school on meeting days. That little brown dress with matching beanie cap made me look like the other Brownie Scouts. I loved that uniform.

In high school, I became a Songleader with pompoms and matching uniforms. By the time I was a senior, everybody could say my name and I felt like I belonged. I was elected Student Body Vice President and voted onto the Homecoming Court.[4] I was taught and I believed I was entitled to all of the rights guaranteed by the U.S. Constitution.

I turned 18 in 1969. The war in Vietnam was raging. Young people like myself were idealistic and full of questions. That year Americans walked on the moon. It was the summer of love and the spirit of Woodstock[5] spread over my generation in a wave of anti-establishment.[6] In 1969, I graduated

---

[1] *Japanese American internment* was the forced removal and containment of approximately 120,000 Japanese and Japanese Americans (more than half of whom were U.S. citizens) from the West Coast of the U.S. during World War II.

[2] *All-American* means a typical American.

[3] *Girl Scouts* is a worldwide organization dedicated to helping girls. For details, go to www.girlscouts.org.

[4] *Homecoming* is a tradition in high schools when graduates are welcomed back. *Homecoming Court* is made up of current students (seniors) elected by their peers to serve as members of the court—King, Queen, and other members.

[5] *Woodstock* refers to the historic Woodstock Rock-n-Roll Festival held in August 1969 in Bethel, New York, which is considered to be one of the greatest moments in music history.

[6] *anti-establishment* refers to a view or belief that goes against the conventional social, political, and economic principles of a society.

from high school in Southern California, I married my surfer boyfriend and we had our first baby on Christmas Day. Many things have happened since those passionate days of my youth. Now I am a Japanese American woman trial attorney representing plaintiffs[7] in discrimination lawsuits against the government. I still believe that everyone is entitled to the civil rights guaranteed by our Constitution. I still believe in my country, with all its imperfections.

Our values of freedom, honesty, diversity and tolerance are our competitive edge in a world that looks to us to see how we live together. We do not hide our problems. We put them on trial and allow everyone to watch how we try to find justice.

I'm no longer an All American girl. I've grown to be a woman professional in a complicated world with shades of gray all around me.

▶ Comprehension Questions

Discuss this story in pairs or small groups.

1. What happened to Patricia's grandparents?

2. What were some of Patricia's activities while in school?

3. What was important about Patricia's uniform?

4. Whom did Patricia marry?

5. What does Patricia do now?

6. What does Patricia think is important about the U.S.?

7. What was the most interesting point for you in this reading?

---

[7] *plaintiffs* means persons who bring action in a court of law.

Cultural Application

The majority of U.S. Americans are quite patriotic about the United States. You might see this exhibited in several ways—the Pledge of Allegiance said each morning by school children at the start of their school day, the U.S. national anthem being played at the start of most sporting events, the colors of the U.S. flag on clothing, the U.S. flag flown at places of business, patriotic bumper stickers on cars, patriotic songs on the radio, and so on. It's a good idea for you to become familiar with the words to the U.S. national anthem and Pledge of Allegiance as well as some of the customs associated with that, such as not wearing a hat when those are being observed or placing one's right hand over one's heart (and standing up) when the U.S. national anthem is being performed.

▼ Vocabulary Exercise

These words appeared in the reading. This activity helps you see how well you understood the vocabulary words. Circle the answer that most closely matches the meaning of the word. If there are any you don't know, add them to your vocabulary notebook.

1. **released**

   I was born in 1951, 6 years after my family was released from the Japanese American Internment Camps.

   released means

   a. locked up

   b. not freed

   c. freed

   d. kept

2. **guaranteed**

   . . . and I believed I was entitled to all of the rights guaranteed by the U.S. Constitution.

   guaranteed means

   a. stopped

   b. blocked

   c. promised

   d. not promised

3. **idealistic**

Young people like myself were idealistic and full of questions.

idealistic means

a. negative

b. real

c. practical

d. full of dreams

4. **still**

I still believe that everyone is entitled to the civil rights. . . .

still means

a. peaceful

b. without motion

c. to continue

d. loud

5. **complicated**

I've grown to be a woman professional in a complicated world with shades of gray all around me.

complicated means

a. complex

b. simple

c. trouble-free

d. not active

▼ Vocabulary Usage

Now, it's your turn to practice using these vocabulary words. Choose at least two vocabulary words, and write your own sentences using these new words in your vocabulary notebook.

▶ Writing/Speaking Practice

Choose one or more of these topics to write about or discuss in pairs or small groups.

1. Describe your grandparents and an experience they had.

2. What is "typical American" in your opinion?

3. What are some differences between the U.S. and another country in regard to laws?

4. How do you feel when you see your country's flag or hear your country's national anthem?

5. Describe your secondary (high) school experience.

▶ Real Life Application: Interacting with U.S. Americans

Activity 1

Ask a few U.S. Americans these questions, and then report back to your class.

1. Tell me about your grandparents and an experience they had.

2. What are some examples of civil rights in this country?

3. Tell me about your high school experience.

4. What is your opinion about the U.S. legal system?

5. What is your overall feeling about the U.S.? How do you feel when you see the U.S. flag or hear the U.S. national anthem?

Activity 2

As you go about your daily life in the next week, look for examples of patriotism (bumper stickers, flags flying, clothing, songs on the radio, etc.), and list what you observe as patriotic examples. Bring your list back to class to share with your classmates.

Activity 3

Watch one of the "High School Musical" movies. Then try to visit a U.S. high school (you need to get permission from the school office first to observe), and write down your observations. Share your observations in class.

Part 2

▼ Pre-Reading Activities

Discuss these questions in pairs or small groups.

1. Find Los Angeles (L.A.) on the map. What do you know about L.A.?

2. Talk about a challenge you have experienced in living in the U.S.

3. What would be difficult for someone about living in your country?

4. What do you think are the most important words in your language? In English?

▼ Vocabulary Prediction

Predict the meaning of these vocabulary words found in the story before you read the story. The word is provided in a sentence or phrase from the story. After you have predicted the meaning, then look up the word in a dictionary, and write the definition.

1. drop-out—*As a high school drop-out at 17, there weren't a lot of people who were there when I needed them.*

   Prediction: A drop-out means _____

   Definition: _____

2. struggling—*When I think of the many times I took the bar exam, struggling to make ends meet. . . .*

   Prediction: Struggling means _____

   Definition: _____

3. bar exam—*When I think of the many times I took the bar exam. . . .*

   Prediction: Bar exam means _____

   Definition: _____

4. encouragement— *. . . I can hear loud and strong my wife's words of encouragement.*

   Prediction: Encouragement means _____

   Definition: _____

Cultural Note: Personal Control, Belief in Self

In the U.S., there is a general belief that people can or should control their own environment and their own futures. Here is a story about a U.S. American who was able to change his future from a high school drop-out to successful lawyer because people communicated how important it was to believe in himself. (On a different note: Notice the reference to making direct eye contact at the end of the story. This was previously discussed in Unit 2.)

James' Story—Los Angeles, California

I have a terrific wife and two great sons. I am a fairly successful lawyer. I have lived in the same house for 16 years and married to the same supportive woman for 25 years. Things are looking pretty good. But it hasn't always been that way.

As a high school drop-out at 17, there weren't a lot of people who were there when I needed them. There weren't a lot of people who believed in me nor did I much believe in myself. As I look back where I came from I can see the faces of people who had faith in me, people who saw things in me that I could not see myself.

The four most powerful words in any language: I believe in you. When as a young man I found myself in Vietnam scared to death of dying I hear the sergeant now: I believe in you. When I felt hopeless and was about to give up ever wanting to be a lawyer, I heard the voice of my father-in-law saying: I believe in you. When I think of the many times I took the bar exam, struggling to make ends meet, I can hear loud and strong my wife's words of encouragement: I believe in you. I have learned over the last 50-plus years that it doesn't really take a lot to give someone the spark they need to get through the tough times . . . All it takes is to look that person in the eye and say "I believe in you"—four simple words that have the power to change lives. It did mine.

▼ Comprehension Questions

Discuss this story in pairs or small groups.

1. Describe James' family.

2. How long has James lived in his house?

3. How long has James been married?

4. What does James do for a job?

5. What happened to James when he was 17?

6. Who or what helped him have faith in himself?

7. What was the most interesting point for you in this reading?

Cultural Application

This is another example of the strong U.S. American belief about the ability to change one's circumstances. In James's situation, he did not finish school but later became successful because other people believed in him and helped him change his situation. Changing one's situation means that it is important to not give up, even when times are difficult. Think about your belief in yourself and others who can support you in trying to achieve your goals. Keep trying.

▶ Vocabulary Exercise

These words appeared in the reading. This activity helps you see how well you understood the vocabulary words. Circle the answer that most closely matches the meaning of the word. If there are any you don't know, add them to your vocabulary notebook.

1. terrific

I have a terrific wife and two great sons.

terrific means

a. wonderful

b. average

c. terrible

d. awful

2. fairly

I am a fairly successful lawyer.

fairly means

a. completely

b. somewhat

c. famously

d. average

3. make ends meet

. . . struggling to make ends meet. . . .

make ends meet means

a. enough money to pay bills

b. wealthy

c. more than enough money to pay bills

d. without money

4. **spark**

. . . it doesn't really take a lot to give someone the spark they need to get through the tough times. . . .

spark means

a. flash

b. to stir to activity

c. inspiring with hope

d. stopping in despair

5. **tough**

. . . the spark they need to get through the tough times.

tough means

a. difficult

b. easy

c. strong

d. weak

▶ Vocabulary Usage

Now, it's your turn to practice using these vocabulary words. Choose at least two vocabulary words, and write your own sentences using these new words in your vocabulary notebook.

▶ Writing/Speaking Practice

Choose one or more of these topics to write about or discuss in pairs or small groups.

1. What has been one challenge you have experienced in living in the U.S.?

2. What gets you through tough times when you may feel like giving up?

3. What do you think are the most important words in your language? In English?

▼ Real Life Application: Interacting with U.S. Americans

Activity 1

Ask a few U.S. Americans these questions, and then report back to your class.

1. Tell me about a challenge you have experienced in living in this country.

2. What gets you through tough times when you may feel like giving up?

3. What do you think are the most important words in English?

4. How important is it to believe in yourself? What advice do you have about believing in yourself?

Activity 2

Choose a biography or autobiography of a U.S. American, and read it. Pay attention to the challenges that person faced and how he or she overcame them. When you are finished, you may want to write a book report and share it with your class. Your teacher can help you know how to write a book report and what information to include. You could also dress up as a character from the book and tell your class about the book from that character's perspective.

▶ End-of-Unit Activities

List at least one new cultural insight you gained from this unit that helps you understand U.S. American culture a little better.

Based on the information in this unit, write at least one or two things you will do or that you want to remember to improve your interactions with U.S. Americans.

Turn to the Notes section at the end of this textbook (page 208), and complete the section related to Unit 12.

A Look at the Northwest

Part 1

▼ **Pre-Reading Activities**

Discuss these questions in pairs or small groups.

1. Find Seattle on a map. Have you been to Seattle or do you know someone who has been there? What do you know about it?

2. How do you make friends?

3. How do U.S. Americans make friends?

4. Talk about friends you have from other cultures.

▼ **Vocabulary Prediction**

Predict the meaning of these vocabulary words found in the story before you read the story. The word is provided in a sentence or phrase from the story. After you have predicted the meaning, then look up the word in a dictionary, and write the definition.

1. **chance meeting**—*Following our chance meeting, we had the opportunity to meet Margaret's family.* . . .

    Prediction: Chance meeting means _____

    Definition: _____

2. **richness**—*Our story includes return visits to Costa Rica, sharing in the richness of the culture.* . . .

    Prediction: Richness means _____

    Definition: _____

3. **inviting**—*We have always enjoyed meeting people and found Margaret and her uncle most inviting.*

   Prediction: **Inviting** means _____

   Definition: _____

Cultural Note: Friendship, American-Style

U.S. Americans often make friends in a casual context and in a relatively short time. It is important not to confuse friendliness with friendship. One of the best ways to make friends with U.S. Americans is by doing activities together. In this story, pay attention to how this friendship started.

Charlotte's Story—Olympia, Washington

My husband Orin and I were traveling in Central America when we met Margaret. She was visiting her uncle and enjoying a picnic lunch in a public park in El Salvador. We have always enjoyed meeting people and found Margaret and her uncle most inviting. Margaret's home country was Costa Rica. Following our chance meeting, we had the opportunity to meet Margaret's family and were warmly welcomed into their country, their home and their lives. Our story includes return visits to Costa Rica, sharing in the richness of the culture and the gift of this international friendship that has spanned more than 40 years. Through all of this we all discovered we are more alike than we are different through our love of and interest in people and our mutual love and respect for each others' cultures.

▶ Comprehension Questions

Discuss this story in pairs or small groups.

1. How did Orin and Charlotte first meet Margaret?

2. What happened after they met?

3. How long did their friendship last?

4. What did they discover in this friendship?

5. How is this friendship similar or different from friendships in your culture?

6. What was the most interesting point for you in this reading?

Cultural Application

In U.S. culture, there is a difference between *friendship* and *friendliness*. Just because someone is friendly to you doesn't mean they will become friends with you. There are also different degrees of friendship in U.S. American culture, from *close friend* to *good friend* to *friend* to *acquaintance*. Don't confuse friendliness with friendship. In the U.S., it may seem easy to become friends, but it may be more difficult to develop a deeper friendship. And remember that there is a saying in the U.S. that "to have friends, you need to first be a friend." So, think about how you can be a friend to others—and in the case of U.S. Americans, this may include doing activities together.

▼ Vocabulary Exercise

These words appeared in the reading. This activity helps you see how well you understood the vocabulary words. Circle the answer that most closely matches the meaning of the word. If there are any you don't know, add them to your vocabulary notebook.

1. **spanned**

   Our story includes . . . the gift of this international friendship that has spanned more than 40 years.

   spanned means

   a. lasted

   b. walked

   c. spun

   d. shortened

2. **mutual**

   Through all of this we all discovered . . . our mutual love . . . for each others' cultures.

   mutual means

   a. divided by both

   b. shared by both

   c. shared by neither

   d. divided by neither

3. **opportunity**

   Following our chance meeting, we had the opportunity to meet Margaret's family. . . .

   opportunity means

   a. a good possibility

   b. a holiday

   c. a bad possibility

   d. a job

4. **respect**

Through all of this we all discovered . . . respect for each others'
cultures.

respect means

a. low opinion

b. interest

c. value

d. disapproval

◤ Vocabulary Usage

Now, it's your turn to practice using these vocabulary words. Choose at least two vocabulary words, and write your own sentences using these new words in your vocabulary notebook.

◤ Writing/Speaking Practice

Choose one or more of these topics to write about or discuss in pairs or small groups.

1. Describe a special friend you have. Describe this friend and how you met. Share what you like to do together.

2. Describe your impressions of friendship in the United States. How is it similar or different from friendship in other cultures?

3. How do you think U.S. Americans make friends? How do you meet someone and become friends?

4. What does it mean to welcome others into your life? How can you welcome others into your life?

5. Explain ways you can be a friend to someone. What is important in being a friend? What is important to you about friendship?

▼ Real Life Application: Interacting with U.S. Americans

Activity 1

Ask a few U.S. Americans these questions, and then report back to your class.

1. How do you meet new people and make friends?

2. What is important to you in a friendship?

3. What do you like to do together with your friends?

4. What advice would you give to someone who wants to become friends with U.S. Americans?

Activity 2

Observe Americans who are friends at the mall, in a restaurant, at a sporting event, or in another public place. What do you notice? How do they interact with each other? What activities are they doing together? Write your observations, and share them in your class.

Part 2

▼ Pre-Reading Activities

Discuss these questions in pairs or small groups.

1. Find Montana and Utah on the map. What do you know about these states?

2. What is your opinion of volunteers?

3. What do people do in your country when they retire?

4. How often do people move in your country?

5. Have you been to any national parks in the U.S.?

▶ Vocabulary Prediction

Predict the meaning of these vocabulary words found in the story before reading the story. The word is provided in a sentence or phrase from the story. After you have predicted the meaning, then look up the word in a dictionary, and write the definition.

1. retired— . . . *when I retired from fulltime employment.*

    Prediction: Retired means _____

    Definition: _____

2. expeditions—*Here I worked part-time guiding flyfishing expeditions.*

    Prediction: Expeditions mean _____

    Definition: _____

3. national forest—*We have always enjoyed our national forests and national parks . . .*

    Prediction: National forest means _____

    Definition: _____

Cultural Note: Volunteerism

In the U.S., some Americans like to volunteer their time—basically do work without pay—to help others to make a difference, to give back, or to just have something to do. It's a way to give thanks or show gratitude. The story that follows is an example of volunteering.

Wayne's Story—Bozeman, Montana

My name is Wayne. I was born in 1935 in the Midwest.[1] When I was 21 (married), I moved my family to the west coast where we raised our three daughters. When they were in college or had married, we moved to Montana. In Montana, I worked in the snack food business—I loved selling. Through these working years, I had gained two pension plans,[2] plus some savings to support us when I retired from fulltime employment.

We then moved from Montana to Utah. Here I worked part-time guiding flyfishing[3] expeditions. Also we volunteered for the United States Forest Service at a Visitor Information Center in southern Utah. The Forest Service provided us a place to live. We currently are volunteers and really enjoy our volunteer work. We have always enjoyed our national forests and national parks and this provides us an opportunity to do something in return for our great country. We have met a lot of wonderful people doing this. Some have become our best friends.

▼ Comprehension Questions

Discuss this story in pairs or small groups.

1. Where was Wayne born?

2. Where did he move his family?

3. Where did he move after his children left home? Now where does he live?

4. What was Wayne's job?

5. What does Wayne do now?

6. What was the most interesting point for you in this reading?

---

[1] *Midwest* as used here refers to the middle part of the U.S.—Ohio, Indiana, Illinois, Iowa, and Missouri.
[2] *pension plan* refers to money that was saved during working years for retirement.
[3] *flyfishing* is a popular fishing method using artificial flies.

Cultural Application

Volunteerism has long been a part of U.S. American culture. Even from the early days of the country, pioneers worked together to help each other. This spirit of volunteering is based on the value of making life better for others, and it's woven throughout U.S. society. Volunteerism also provides a way to give back—to show one's gratitude for what has been provided. Think about ways you could volunteer and give back to the community.

▶ Vocabulary Exercise

These words appeared in the reading. This activity helps you see how well you understood the vocabulary words. Circle the answer that most closely matches the meaning of the word. If there are any you don't know, add them to your vocabulary notebook.

1. **raised**

   . . . I moved my family to the west coast where we raised our three daughters.

   raised means

   a. grew

   b. increase

   c. to bring up

   d. decreased

2. **gained**

   Through these working years, I had gained two pension plans. . . .

   gained means

   a. lost

   b. found

   c. earned

   d. started

3. **savings**

. . . I had gained two pension plans, plus some savings to support us. . . .

savings means

a. money to spend

b. left-overs

c. money put aside

d. property

4. **employment**

. . . plus some savings to support us when I retired from fulltime employment.

employment means

a. work

b. free time

c. service

d. selling

▶ Vocabulary Usage

Now, it's your turn to practice using these vocabulary words. Choose at least two vocabulary words, and write your own sentences using these new words in your vocabulary notebook.

▶ Writing/Speaking Practice

Choose one or more of these topics to write about or discuss in pairs or small groups.

1. What do you think about volunteering? Have you ever volunteered or do you know others who have? Explain.

2. Describe a natural park to visit in another country.

3. Where have you lived in your lifetime?

4. Based on where you grew up, is it more typical for people to move around or to stay in one place? How is this similar or different in the United States?

5. What do you plan to do when you retire?

▼ Real Life Application: Interacting with U.S. Americans

Activity 1

Ask a few U.S. Americans these questions, and then report back to your class.

1. Have you ever volunteered? Where and why?

2. Where have you lived in the U.S.?

3. What do you plan to do when you retire?

4. Which U.S. national parks would you recommend visiting?

Activity 2

Research national parks in the U.S., and choose one for a poster presentation. Contact the national park, and ask them to send you materials and brochures. Then put this information together in a poster to share with the class.

Activity 3

Make a list of 3 or 4 possible organizations in your community in which to volunteer, and then write a brief summary about each one, including the history of the organization, what the organization does, and volunteer opportunities within the organization. (You can find out this information by searching online, calling an organization like United Way, or calling the organizations directly.) Share these summaries with your class. If you're really interested in volunteering, you may even want to volunteer some time at an organization, which is a great way to help improve your English and to meet other Americans. Even if you don't volunteer, you may want to interview some volunteers to find out more about why they volunteer and to ask them to share with you more about their volunteer experience.

End-of-Unit Activities

List at least one new cultural insight you gained from this unit that helps you understand U.S. American culture a little better.

Based on the information in this unit, write at least one or two things that you will do or that you want to remember to improve your interactions with U.S. Americans.

Turn to the Notes section at the end of this textbook (page 209), and complete the section related to Unit 13.

A Look at Hawaii and Alaska

Part 1

▶ Pre-Reading Activities

Discuss these questions in pairs or small groups.

1. Find Hawaii on the map. What do you know about Hawaii?

2. How did you come to live where you do now? Where is your family from originally?

3. Why do people move to other countries? Explain and give an example, if you can.

▶ Vocabulary Prediction

Predict the meaning of these vocabulary words found in the story before you read the story. The word is provided in a sentence or phrase from the story. After you have predicted the meaning, then look up the word in a dictionary and write the definition.

1. **heterogeneous**—*Our island population is so heterogeneous and intermarried. . . .*

   Prediction: Heterogeneous means_____

   Definition: _____

2. **derogatory**— *. . . we're careful to not be derogatory of any race. . . .*

   Prediction: Derogatory means _____

   Definition: _____

3. standard— . . . *I believe we (Hawaii) set the standard for ethnic diversity and racial tolerance.*

Prediction: Standard means _____

Definition: _____

Cultural Note: Equality in Diversity

The U.S. has a diverse mix of people and, in general, Americans embrace multiculturalism. Two stories that share more about that diversity follow.

Frank's Story—Honolulu, Hawaii

I write from Hawaii, from the shores of the western most state of the Union. My family has now been Americans for over a century, my grandfather arriving from China in 1885 to labor in the pineapple fields. Our family is typical of immigrants who came to Hawaii. Our island population is so heterogeneous and intermarried, so we're careful to not be derogatory of any race since we might well be speaking about our cousins, in-laws, husbands and wives. Indeed, in Hawaii we celebrate the traditions of others with annual festivals from many different cultures. Here in Hawaii, the rainbow in the sky, reflected in the faces of our people, is our symbol of the promise of Aloha[1] extended to new arrivals. Though America still has racial stumbling blocks, I believe we (Hawaii) set the standard for ethnic diversity and racial tolerance.

---

[1] *Aloha* is the way people of Hawaii say "Hello" and "Welcome" in native Hawaiian.

▛ Comprehension Questions

Discuss this story in pairs or small groups.

1. Where is Frank's family from?

2. When did Frank's family arrive in Hawaii?

3. What did Frank's grandfather do?

4. What does Frank think about immigrants in Hawaii?

5. How do people in Hawaii celebrate the traditions of others?

6. What was the most interesting point for you in this reading?

▛ Reading Comprehension: True or False?

Read the sentences, and decide whether they are true or false based on the information in the story. Write T for true or F for false.

_____ 1. Frank's grandfather came from Japan.

_____ 2. Frank's family has been in Hawaii for 50 years.

_____ 3. Hawaii is not very diverse.

_____ 4. Hawaiians celebrate the cultural traditions of many different cultures.

_____ 5. Aloha means "Hello and Welcome."

▌ Vocabulary Exercise

These words appeared in the reading. This activity helps you see how well you understood the vocabulary words. Circle the answer that most closely matches the meaning of the word. If there are any you don't know, add them to your vocabulary notebook.

1. **reflected**

   Here in Hawaii, the rainbow in the sky, reflected in the faces of our people. . . .

   reflected means
   a. reproduced
   b. thought
   c. felt
   d. shown

2. **extended**

   . . . is our symbol of the promise of Aloha extended to new arrivals.

   extended means
   a. lengthened
   b. offered
   c. not granted
   d. stretched

3. **stumbling blocks**

   Though America still has racial stumbling blocks. . . .

   stumbling blocks means
   a. stepping stones
   b. obstacles that make you fall
   c. smooth climbing
   d. obstacles to further progress

4. tolerance

. . . I believe we (Hawaii) set the standard for ethnic diversity and racial tolerance.

tolerance means

a. no acceptance

b. open-mindedness

c. not caring

d. narrow-mindedness

▶ Vocabulary Usage

Now, it's your turn to practice using these vocabulary words. Choose at least two vocabulary words, and write your own sentences using these new words in your vocabulary notebook.

▶ Writing/Speaking Practice

Choose one or more of these topics to write about or discuss in pairs or small groups.

1. Describe some different cultures found in another country or in the U.S.

2. Describe some people you have met in the U.S. from different backgrounds.

3. What are some ways to celebrate cultural diversity?

4. What are some stumbling blocks to accepting people from other cultural backgrounds and some ways to overcome those stumbling blocks?

▼ Real Life Application: Interacting with U.S. Americans

Activity 1

Ask a few U.S. Americans these questions, and then report back to your class.

1. Where is your family from originally?

2. What is your opinion of racial tolerance in the U.S.?

3. What do you think some racial stumbling blocks are in the U.S.?

4. What ideas do you have for overcoming these stumbling blocks?

Activity 2

Read the local newspapers and research on the Internet about ways in which your local community celebrates other cultures. Look for cultural festivals, concerts, etc., and make a list to share with your class.

Activity 3

Attend a community event that is intended to celebrate a culture found in your community; examples include an African American music concert or a cultural festival that celebrates another culture. Write about your experience.

Part 2

▼ Pre-Reading Activities

Discuss these questions in pairs or small groups.

1. Find Alaska on a map. What do you know about Alaska?

2. When you meet people who look different from you, what do you think?

3. What have been others' responses to you when they meet you?

▼ Vocabulary Prediction

Predict the meaning of these vocabulary words found in the story before you read the story. The word is provided in a sentence or phrase from the story. After you have predicted the meaning, then look up the word in a dictionary, and write the definition.

1. **classically**—*My skin is darker and my features aren't classically Caucasian.*

   Prediction: Classically means_____

   Definition: _____

2. **private sector**— *. . . I moved to the private sector, got a job. . . .*

   Prediction: Private sector means _____

   Definition: _____

3. **appearance**—*As a kid, I never thought about my outside appearance.*

   Prediction: Appearance means _____

   Definition: _____

4. **ability**—*Our greatest strength is in our ability to embrace all people and make them our own.*

   Prediction: Ability means _____

   Definition: _____

Michael's Story—Anchorage, Alaska

I am an American. Others just looking at me might not see that at first. My skin is darker and my features aren't classically Caucasian. I was born in Cheyenne, Wyoming. I grew up there and in Alaska. I graduated high school in Anchorage and joined the Navy. After 6 years in the submarine force, I moved to the private sector, got a job, and raised a family. In the Navy, I toured the world and each society I visited seemed easier for me to integrate than for my buddies on the boat. I was almost more comfortable away than at home. As a kid, I never thought about my outside appearance. Now, I realize it's always been an issue for others. It makes me wonder how my opportunities in life have been affected. When I go to the airport today, security looks at me longer. It's okay. My life mirrors millions of others in this country. I'm a son of immigrants with a foot in two worlds, but with an added twist. My immigrant German mother worked as a cleaning woman on a Cheyenne air force base. My Saudi Arabian father was in military training there. After I was born, my father returned to Saudi Arabia and I've never had any contact with him. So I grew up (American). My mom and grandparents with their German accents raised me and must have dealt with issues too, tagging me along in the 50s. Looking at things now, I believe that unless you're born to one of the first nations of this continent, all modern Americans are some kind of immigrant. Our greatest strength is in our ability to embrace all people and make them our own.

▶ Comprehension Questions

Discuss this story in pairs or small groups.

1. Where was Michael born?

2. Where were Michael's parents from, and what were their jobs?

3. What did Michael do after he graduated from high school?

4. What happened to Michael's father?

5. What happens when Michael goes to the airport and why?

6. What does Michael believe is Americans' greatest strength?

7. What other comments do you have after reading about Michael's experiences?

8. What was the most interesting point for you in this reading?

Reading Comprehension: True or False?

Read the sentences, and decide whether they are true or false based on the information in the story. Write T for true or F for false.

_____ 1. Both of Michael's parents were from Germany.

_____ 2. Michael was in the U.S. Navy for 6 years.

_____ 3. Michael raised a family.

_____ 4. Michael has not traveled very much.

_____ 5. Michael feels more comfortable when he is not in the U.S.

_____ 6. Michael believes that all modern Americans are immigrants.

Cultural Application

The United States is quite diverse in its population and in the various cultures represented. While many Americans embrace diversity and multiculturalism, you may encounter some Americans who are still quite protective of their own culture and may respond in more negative ways toward those from different cultural backgrounds. Be prepared to encounter a variety of responses from different Americans, always treating each person with respect, regardless of how they respond to you.

▼ Vocabulary Exercise

These words appeared in the reading. This activity helps you see how well you understood the vocabulary words. Circle the answer that most closely matches the meaning of the word. If there are any you don't know, add them to your vocabulary notebook.

1. integrate

   . . . each society I visited seemed easier for me to integrate than for my buddies on the boat.

   integrate means
   a. disconnect
   b. divide
   c. separate
   d. to become part of

2. issue

   Now, I realize it's always been an issue for others.

   issue means
   a. newspaper
   b. thought
   c. problem
   d. item

3. twist

I'm a son of immigrants with a foot in two worlds, but with an added twist.

twist means

a. to straighten

b. a curve

c. an unexpected event

d. link

4. contact

. . . and I've never had any contact with him.

contact means

a. meeting

b. communication

c. touching

d. separation

5. embrace

Our greatest strength is in our ability to embrace all people and make them our own.

embrace means

a. welcome

b. reject

c. accept

d. exclude

▼ Vocabulary Usage

Now, it's your turn to practice using these vocabulary words. Choose at least two vocabulary words, and write your own sentences using these new words in your vocabulary notebook.

▶ Writing/Speaking Practice

Choose one or more of these topics to write about or discuss in pairs or small groups.

1. Describe some of the places you have traveled to—what were your favorite places? Where did you feel most comfortable, and why?

2. What has it been like for you to live in the U.S.? What has been easy for you? What has been difficult?

3. Do you feel Americans embrace diversity? Why or why not?

4. What do you feel Americans' greatest strength is?

▶ Real Life Application: Interacting with U.S. Americans

Activity 1

Ask a few U.S. Americans these questions, and then report back to your class.

1. Where have you traveled in the United States? Which places do you recommend to visit?

2. How can Americans embrace immigrants?

3. What do you think the greatest strength is of the American people?

Activity 2

Find a newspaper article (or an online article) about immigrants, write a summary about the article, and bring it to class.

Activity 3

Find a place in your community (flea market, church, ethnic grocery store, restaurant) where you might see some immigrants. If possible, visit this place and talk with some of the persons you meet there about their experiences living in the U.S. Report your findings back to your class.

▶ End-of-Unit Activities

List at least one new cultural insight you gained from this unit that helps you understand U.S. American culture a little better.

Based on the information in this unit, write one or two things that you will do or that you want to remember that will improve your interactions with U.S. Americans.

Turn to the Notes section at the end of this textbook (page 209), and complete the section related to Unit 14.

Conclusion: Understanding U.S. American Culture

Part 1

▶ Pre-Reading Activities

Discuss these questions in pairs or small groups.

1. What impressions do you have about U.S. American culture from American movies and television? How typical do you think these impressions are of U.S. American culture?

2. What does it mean to "tolerate something"? What are some things you tolerate?

3. How do you feel about differences? About people who are different from you?

▶ Vocabulary Prediction

Predict the meaning of these vocabulary words found in the story before you read the story. The word is provided in a sentence or phrase from the story. After you have predicted the meaning, then look up the word in a dictionary, and write the definition.

1. **ancestry**—*My grandparents with their Native American ancestry. . . .*

   Prediction: Ancestry means _____

   Definition: _____

2. veteran—*I am myself a Veteran of the United States Marine Corps. . . .*

   Prediction: Veteran means _____

   Definition: _____

3. mercy—*Not FOX News Moslems, but Islaam seen as a mercy to mankind.*

   Prediction: Mercy means _____

   Definition: _____

4. toiled—*. . . were paid nearly nothing and eventually owning the almost 100 acres they toiled.*

   Prediction: Toiled means _____

   Definition: _____

Cultural Note: Embracing Difference, Focus on the Future

The United States has a history of people from diverse backgrounds coming together and interacting to create a single country. How is it that persons from different cultures, religions, and backgrounds can live, work, and play together? Here's a story about one U.S. American's experience with difference and his hope in how we can embrace difference as we move forward into our future together.

Reginald's Story—Raleigh, North Carolina

I am a product of tolerance. My grandparents with their Native American ancestry, who sharecropped[1] for years, were paid nearly nothing and eventually owning the almost 100 acres they toiled.

My first-generation college-grad mother attended a segregated[2] university at the height of the Civil Rights Movement.[3] My father (whose father had been lynched[4] when he was a child) at that same time, fought in the US Army during Vietnam. I am All-American . . . but it does not make me bitter—it makes me tolerant. It makes me better able to process the feelings of being and nothingness, of ownership and being disowned, of truly understanding the term, "you're either with us, or against us." This is My America.

I am myself a Veteran of the United States Marine Corps, who knows full well the value of blood, honor and the hard-fought freedoms I espouse.[5] My wife's family is Garifuna from Central America, so we speak in our home, a strange mélange[6] of English, Fusha, Afro-Latin and Southeastern Region Bluesese.[7] She was once Roman Catholic, and I Southern Baptist, until we both came to understand the universal truths of Islaam, though strange and misunderstood in this land. Not FOX News[8] Moslems, but

---

[1] *sharecrop* means living and working on someone else's land and giving a share of the crops to the owner in lieu of rent. This was practiced in the U.S. following the Civil War through the early 20th century.

[2] *segregated* means separate—in the U.S. in the first half of the 20th century blacks and whites were segregated in public.

[3] *Civil Rights Movement* in the U.S. was led by Martin Luther King, Jr., in the 1950s and 1960s and sought more rights for African Americans.

[4] *lynch* means to kill someone, usually a mob killing by hanging without a fair trial. Lynching was used by whites to kill African Americans in the first half of the 20th century in the U.S.

[5] *espouse* means support.

[6] *melange* means mix.

[7] *Bluesese* is an unofficial term used to describe a dialect, often spoken by African Americans in the southeastern U.S.

[8] *FOX News* is a conservative TV channel in the U.S.

Islaam seen as a mercy to mankind. My wife and I—we have a unique perception as Americans, of how we are perceived from the inside and out. This is Our America.

We understand our sameness and differences. America is what it is due to these differences, all of its tolerances and intolerances, its separatism and equalities. Though we are seen across the world as this singular Hollywood-inspired mega-culture, America is as different in opinion as indigenous population's first sight of an explorer on her shores. Her perceptions are as varied as stepping onto Plymouth Rock[9] or surviving the Middle Passage.[10] In America, if there is nothing else that you learn, the most important thing will be: Don't simply be tolerant—Understand, embrace, and know difference. This is Your America.

Comprehension Questions

Discuss this story in pairs or small groups.

1. Describe Reginald's grandparents. What were their backgrounds? What did they do?

2. Describe Reginald's parents.

3. How does Reginald feel about tolerance?

4. What is Reginald's background?

5. What is Reginald's wife's background?

6. What is the most important thing to learn about America, according to Reginald?

7. What was the most interesting point for you in this reading?

---

[9] *Plymouth Rock* is referring to the Pilgrims that came from England in 1621.
[10] *Middle Passage* refers to forced transportation of African people from Africa to the New World as part of the Atlantic slave trade during the 16th to 18th centuries—at least 1 million lost their lives during the ocean journey to the New World.

Cultural Application

This story illustrates how U.S. Americans come from many different backgrounds and yet see themselves as "Americans." Within U.S. culture, there is a continued focus on the future and how U.S. Americans can make the future better by allowing differences to be a strength. Think about your role in helping to make a better future in this society—in helping others understand and embrace difference, of how to treat others with respect and acceptance, of being open to new ideas. Don't be afraid to take risks. Seek ways to overcome your challenges, and seek people who can help you do that. Be enthusiastic about solving problems in your own life and in your community. Build relationships with those who are different—we all share the future.

▌ Vocabulary Exercise

These words appeared in the reading. This activity helps you see how well you understood the vocabulary words. Circle the answer that most closely matches the meaning of the word. If there are any you don't know, add them to your vocabulary notebook.

1. **bitter**

   I am All-American . . . but it does not make me bitter. . . .

   bitter means
   a. pleasant
   b. peaceful
   c. sweet
   d. resentful

2. **universal**

   . . . until we both came to understand the universal truths of Islaam. . . .

   universal means
   a. common to all
   b. limited
   c. narrow
   d. special

3. **perceived**

. . . of how we are perceived from the inside and out.

perceived means

a. seen

b. not noticed

c. noted

d. overlooked

4. **process**

It makes me better able to process the feelings of being. . . .

process means

a. to think about, analyze

b. to remember

c. to talk about

d. to write

▨ Vocabulary Usage

Now, it's your turn to practice using these vocabulary words. Choose at least two vocabulary words, and write your own sentences using these new words in your vocabulary notebook.

▨ Writing/Speaking Practice

Choose one or more of these topics to write about or discuss in pairs or small groups.

1. What do you think is the most important thing to learn or know about the United States?

2. What do you think is the most important thing to learn or know about another country?

3. Describe what "America" is to you. How would you describe your experience in the U.S.? What are some highlights and what has been difficult?

4. How can people move beyond tolerance to truly understand each other?

5. What excites you about the future?

◤ Real Life Application: Interacting with U.S. Americans

Activity 1

Ask a few U.S. Americans these questions, and then report back to your class.

1. What do you think is most important to know about the U.S. culture?

2. What do you think life is like for minorities in the U.S.?

3. How can people from different cultures truly embrace and understand each other?

4. What excites you about the future?

Activity 2

Research more about how African Americans have been treated in the United States. Try to learn more about slavery in the U.S., about Jim Crow laws or about the Civil Rights Movement in the U.S. You can find this information on the Internet and in the library.

Activity 3

Find out more about multiculturalism in the U.S. and what is being done to help people from different cultures understand each other better. What kind of training or classes are available in your community on this topic (other related topics include diversity, cross-cultural communication, and culture-specific topics)? What books are available? What can you do in the community to help U.S. Americans better understand other cultures about which you are knowledgeable?

Part 2

Your Story

Now it's your turn to write a brief story about something that is important to you in your own culture, following a format similar to the stories you've read in this textbook. Here are some questions to consider as you write your story:

Your name: ______________________________

Your cultural background: ______________________________

Title of your story: ______________________________

Write your story in the space provided. You can include a memory, something you believe in, an underlying cultural value that is important to you, something that is very important for others to know and understand about you and your cultural background, and so on.

____

____

____

____

____

____

____

____

____

____

____

____

____

▟ Reading Comprehension

Write three questions about your story that you would like readers to answer.

1. _____

2. _____

3. _____

▟ Vocabulary Exercise

Write at least three words from your story that readers may not know. Write a definition of those words.

1. _____

2. _____

3. _____

▟ Vocabulary Usage

Now, it's your turn to practice using these vocabulary words. Choose at least two vocabulary words, and write new sentences (not from your story) using these words in your vocabulary notebook.

Writing/Speaking Practice

Share your story with your classmates. Listen to the stories that your classmates read. As you listen, pay attention to new words you do not know. Also listen for the main points of each story regarding what is important culturally to your classmates. Write your notes below as you listen to your classmates' personal stories.

New Vocabulary Words	Personal Stories: Main Points

Vocabulary Usage

Now, it's your turn to practice using these vocabulary words. Choose at least two vocabulary words, and write your own sentences using these new words in your vocabulary notebook.

▶ Concluding Activities

Reflection Questions

After working through this book, you hopefully have gained a better understanding of U.S. American culture. As you think back on the stories you've read and the notes you kept regarding the cultural values discussed, reflect on these questions, and then discuss these in pairs or small groups:

1. What are some of the themes (values) that you read more than once?

2. What would you say are some of the main values in U.S. American culture, based on these readings and your interactions with U.S. Americans?

3. How would you describe U.S. American culture now?

4. What will you do differently now when you interact with U.S. Americans so that you can be more effective and appropriate in your interactions with them?

▶ Action Ideas

After you reflect on and discuss these questions, take some time to do these activities.

1. Develop your own action plan for key points you want to remember when you interact with U.S. Americans so you will be more effective and appropriate in your interactions with them. Use the notes you made to develop this action plan (see page 200).

2. Write a letter to someone from your culture (or another culture) about U.S. American culture, based on what you've learned.

3. Create a collage about U.S American culture using photos, magazine ads, newspaper headlines, and so on that represent the values highlighted in the textbook that would give a more holistic representation of U.S. American culture.

4. Write an essay about the differences and similarities between another culture and U.S. American culture and ideas you have about better understanding each other.

5. Find a topic in the newspaper or online that seems to be important to U.S. Americans and discuss this issue from a U.S. American perspective, based on what you've learned through this textbook about U.S. American culture.

6. Work with your classmates to write a play about U.S. American culture that illustrates some of the cultural patterns discussed in this textbook.

7. Start an online blog about your experiences of daily life in your community.

8. Start a book club with members from different cultures and read books by authors from different cultures.

9. Using a disposable (or digital) camera, take photos of your community and daily life that illustrate the different cultures in your community (or you could choose to focus on one culture). Then put these together in a booklet and write descriptions about how these photos relate to your understanding of other cultures.

10. Your own ideas: _____

▶ My Action Plan

Write at least one action idea you will do to help you be more successful interacting with U.S. Americans. Include a timeline for what you need to do, beginning with the next steps to take. Share this with your classmates and teacher.

_____

_____

_____

_____

_____

_____

▶ End-of-Unit Activities

List at least one new cultural insight you gained from this unit that helps you understand U.S. American culture a little better.

_____

_____

_____

Based on the information in this unit, write at least one or two things that you will do or that you want to remember to improve your interactions with U.S. Americans.

_____

_____

_____

Turn to the Notes section at the end of this textbook (page 210), and complete the section related to Unit 15.

Notes Section

This is the section where you will record your reflections after you read each story. This reflection time may not be easy and may take some time but it is very important for you to spend enough time in thinking about this. The time you spend thinking about what this means will help make you more successful in interacting with U.S. Americans. When you complete this textbook, you will have all of your notes here in one place to allow for further reflection and provide you with what you need to complete the concluding activities.

Instructions

You are asked to write in the U.S. American cultural pattern or value found in the story in the first column for each of the units. In the second column, you are asked to think about what this pattern looks like in your own upbringing—in other words, what you were taught as a child about this. This may be similar to the cultural pattern found in the story or it may be completely opposite. Take some time to think about what you were taught as a child, and then write your response in the second column. For example, perhaps one of the stories illustrates the concept of "individualism" in U.S. culture. In your own upbringing, perhaps you were taught more about "importance of group." So, in that case, in you would write "importance of the group" in the second column. In the third column, you need to take some time to reflect about the impact of the U.S. cultural pattern on people's behaviors in the United States—how do many U.S. Americans behave as a result of this U.S. cultural pattern or value? You can also write something you think is important to remember in regard to this cultural pattern—perhaps a way that you need to adapt your own behavior in order to be more successful in relating to U.S. Americans around this particular pattern or value.

Note: As you reflect, please remember that these stories in this textbook represent cultural patterns found in U.S. American culture and that while many U.S. Americans you meet will fit these patterns, there will be some who do not fit these patterns at all. Patterns can help you try to understand behaviors you encounter in U.S. American culture. However, since not everyone will ~~'~~hose patterns, it is most important that you get to know each person and ~~'~~stand their unique backgrounds and experiences.

Unit 1

Personal Story	U.S. American Cultural Pattern/ Value in the Story	Cultural Pattern/ Value in My Upbringing	Impact of U.S. Cultural Pattern/What I Need to Remember
Tonu's Story			
Viviana's Story			

Unit 2

Personal Story	U.S. American Cultural Pattern/ Value in the Story	Cultural Pattern/ Value in My Upbringing	Impact of U.S. Cultural Pattern/What I Need to Remember
Matt's Story			

Unit 3

Personal Story	U.S. American Cultural Pattern/ Value in the Story	Cultural Pattern/ Value in My Upbringing	Impact of U.S. Cultural Pattern/What I Need to Remember
Kate's Story			
Maria's Story			

Unit 2

Unit 4

Personal Story	U.S. American Cultural Pattern/ Value in the Story	Cultural Pattern/ Value in My Upbringing	Impact of U.S. Cultural Pattern/What I Need to Remember
Lawrence's Story			
Julu's Story			

Unit 5

Personal Story	U.S. American Cultural Pattern/ Value in the Story	Cultural Pattern/ Value in My Upbringing	Impact of U.S. Cultural Pattern/What I Need to Remember
Helen's Story			
Megan's Story			

Unit 6

Personal Story	U.S. American Cultural Pattern/ Value in the Story	Cultural Pattern/ Value in My Upbringing	Impact of U.S. Cultural Pattern/What I Need to Remember
Kay's Story			
Kim's Story			

Unit 7

Personal Story	U.S. American Cultural Pattern/ Value in the Story	Cultural Pattern/ Value in My Upbringing	Impact of U.S. Cultural Pattern/What I Need to Remember
Becky's Story			
Steve's Story			

Unit 8

Personal Story	U.S. American Cultural Pattern/ Value in the Story	Cultural Pattern/ Value in My Upbringing	Impact of U.S. Cultural Pattern/What I Need to Remember
Stephen's Story			
Shirley's Story			

Unit 9

Personal Story	U.S. American Cultural Pattern/ Value in the Story	Cultural Pattern/ Value in My Upbringing	Impact of U.S. Cultural Pattern/What I Need to Remember
Hannah's Story			
Amber's Story			

Unit 10

Personal Story	U.S. American Cultural Pattern/ Value in the Story	Cultural Pattern/ Value in My Upbringing	Impact of U.S. Cultural Pattern/What I Need to Remember
Edith's Story			
A-Jamal's Story			

Unit 11

Personal Story	U.S. American Cultural Pattern/ Value in the Story	Cultural Pattern/ Value in My Upbringing	Impact of U.S. Cultural Pattern/What I Need to Remember
Marlene's Story			
Arlene's Story			

Unit 12

Personal Story	U.S. American Cultural Pattern/ Value in the Story	Cultural Pattern/ Value in My Upbringing	Impact of U.S. Cultural Pattern/What I Need to Remember
Patricia's Story			
James' Story			

Unit 13

Personal Story	U.S. American Cultural Pattern/ Value in the Story	Cultural Pattern/ Value in My Upbringing	Impact of U.S. Cultural Pattern/What I Need to Remember
Charlotte's Story			
Wayne's Story			

Unit 14

Personal Story	U.S. American Cultural Pattern/ Value in the Story	Cultural Pattern/ Value in My Upbringing	Impact of U.S. Cultural Pattern/What I Need to Remember
Frank's Story			
Michael's Story			

Unit 15

Personal Story	U.S. American Cultural Pattern/ Value in the Story	Cultural Pattern/ Value in My Upbringing	Impact of U.S. Cultural Pattern/What I Need to Remember
Reginald's Story			